long. 68°
lat. 45°
BAY
Whiting Bay
Lubec
Johnson Bay
Federal Harbor, Denbow Neck
West Quoddy Head
South Trescott
Machias
River
Narraguagus
Machias
Machiasport
Bucks Hbr.
Machias Bay
Cutler
Eastern Knubble
Little River I.
GRAND
GRAND MANAN CHANNEL
Roque Island
Starboard
Cross I.
Western Head
Englishman Bay
River
Milbridge
Addison
Jonesport
Bunker Hole
Reach
Beals
Moosabec
Trafton I.
Narraguagus Bay
Great Wass Island
Machias Seal I.
Ellsworth
Union River Bay
Surry
Morgan Bay
BLUE HILL MTN
Blue Hill
Blue Hill Harbor
Bagaduce River
Brooksville
Waukeag Neck
Gouldsboro
Sorrento
Prospect Harbor
Porcupine Is.
Grindstone Neck
Gouldsboro Bay
Corea
Winter Harbor
Schoodic Pt.
SCHOODIC PENINSULA
Petit Manan I.
Bartlett I.
Bar Harbor
CADILLAC MTN
MT. DESERT ISLAND
Somes Sound
Northeast Harbor
Southwest Harbor
Otter Cliffs
FRENCHMAN BAY
BLUE HILL BAY
Brooklin
Reach
DEER ISLE
Hadlock Cove
Islesford
Little Cranberry
Baker I.
Bass Harbor
Great Cranberry I.
CRANBERRY ISLES
Casco Passage
Buckle I.
Thorofare
JERICHO BAY
SWANS ISLAND
Lunt Harbor
Frenchboro
Merchant Row
Burnt Coat Hbr.
Hockamock Head
Frenchboro Long Island
BAY
ISLE AU HAUT
Maine
of
OCEAN

The ROCKBOUND COAST

Travels in Maine

The ROCKBOUND COAST

Travels in Maine

BY

Christopher Little

W · W · NORTON & COMPANY

NEW YORK · LONDON

FIRST EDITION

The text of this book is composed in Avanta with the display set in Craw Modern Bold and Boulevard. Composition and manufacturing by The Haddon Craftsmen. Book design by Marjorie J. Flock.

Library of Congress Cataloging-in-Publication Data

Little, Christopher.
The rockbound coast: travels in Maine / by Christopher Little.
p. cm.
Includes bibliographical references (p.).
1. Maine—Description and travel. 2. Atlantic Coast (Me.)—Description and travel. 3. Sailing—Maine—Atlantic Coast. 4. Little, Christopher—Journeys—Maine—Atlantic Coast. 5. Atlantic Coast (Me.)—Pictorial works. I. Title.
F26.L58 1994
917.4104'43—dc20 94-4396

ISBN 0-393-03635-9

W. W. Norton & Company, Inc., 500 Fifth Avenue, New York, N.Y. 10110
W. W. Norton & Company Ltd., 10 Coptic Street, London WC1A 1PU

1 2 3 4 5 6 7 8 9 0

Frederick Goodrich Crane
1923–1992

CONTENTS

ACKNOWLEDGMENTS

I AM CHIEFLY INDEBTED TO Fred and Joyce Crane, the owners of the sloop *Consolation,* who loaned us their most prized possession and, along with her, their selfless and unflagging support for this project.

In Dicken Crane—my *Captain Courageous*—I could not have found a more enthusiastic or patient companion had I scoured the oceans of the world. Thanks, Dicken, for your indefatigable "Yo-ho-ho!" To my sometimes crewmates, Coe Kittredge, "Fitz" Fitzpatrick, Carrie Crane, and Chuck Chadwick, thank you for all your anchor-yanking and bonhomie.

My thanks also go to those whose individual generosities made this book a reality: Stuart and Anastazia Little; Philip Conkling of the Island Institute; Mallory Mercaldi; Nellie Blagden; Walter Lord; M.C. Marden; Tom and Kate Chappell; Irving Slavid; Cricket Lyman; Jamie, Toshiko, and Tei Carpenter; Hannah Batchelder; Michael Mahan; Co Crocker; Charles Foote of Camden Marine; Angela Drexel; and Jay Espy of the Maine Coast Heritage Trust. Many thanks to the librarians of the Norfolk (Connecticut) Library, who collectively suffered aphasia whenever my research books came due, and especially to Jan and the late Hank Taft, coauthors of *A Cruising Guide to the Maine Coast,* whose knowledgeable pathfinding made more than one tricky harbor easier to enter.

Had it not been for William F. Buckley, Jr., and the great adventures portrayed in *Atlantic High, Racing Through Paradise,* and *WindFall,* the seed for this book might never have been sown. Characteristically, WFB, your enthusiasm was infectious.

To my agent, Angela Miller: thanks for getting me a date with James Mairs. To Jim Mairs, Senior Editor at W. W. Norton, I thank you for your astute counsel. And to Cecil Lyon, Jim Mairs's astute *counselor:* would you mind if I put in an early nomination for your beatification?

All those mentioned above are in every sense coconspirators, but only up to the point of errors and omissions. For those inevitable faux pas, I alone am to blame.

I send special thanks to my permanent crewmates, Betsy and Eliza. Their enthusiasm during the trip made getting up before dawn a little easier; their patience during the grumpiest moments of my writing made my respect and love for them soar.

Consolation is a sailboat, whom you will get to know in the pages of this book. While it may seem strange, I think of her as every bit as much of a character as the people depicted herein. With that in mind, I say: *Consolation,* you took us everywhere we wanted to go safely, speedily, and, above all, stylishly. Thank you so very much. No, *Hoggie,* I haven't forgotten you. Thank you, too.

C.S.V.L.

Colebrook, Connecticut

On November 22, 1992, only a few weeks after Fred Crane read the manuscript for this book, he died from injuries sustained in a logging accident. If there was anything Fred loved as much as *Consolation* and the coast of Maine, it was working in the woods of his beloved Holiday Farm in Dalton, Massachusetts.

The funeral service was held on the day after Thanksgiving. His four children—Carrie, Timmy, Mary, and Dicken—and his daughter-in-law, Patty, all spoke powerfully of the vibrant, happy man we will so sorely miss. Each in his own way spoke of Fred as the consummate outdoorsman—sailor, skier, birder, woodsman.

After the brave eulogies and before the tearful singing of "The Navy Hymn" (". . . Oh hear us when we cry to thee,/For those in peril on the sea."), the minister read the poem "Sea-Fever."

> I must go down to the seas again, to the lonely sea and the sky,
> And all I ask is a tall ship and a star to steer her by,
> And the wheel's kick and the wind's song and the white sail's shaking,
> And a grey mist on the sea's face and a grey dawn breaking.
>
> I must go down to the seas again, for the call of the running tide
> Is a wild call and a clear call that may not be denied.
> And all I ask is a windy day with the white clouds flying,
> And the flying spray and the blown spume, and the sea-gulls crying.
>
> I must go down to the seas again, to the vagrant gypsy life,
> To the gull's way and the whale's way where the wind's like a whetted knife;
> And all I ask is a merry yarn from a laughing fellow-rover,
> And quiet sleep and a sweet dream when the long trick's over.

Through my own tears, it struck me that Masefield's poem was so to the point—particularly that final stanza—that he might have written it especially for Fred . . . except for one thing: Fred's "trick" wasn't quite long enough.

The ROCKBOUND COAST

Travels in Maine

PROLOGUE

THE WIND had backed around to the southwest, and *Consolation* was bounding along before a following sea, sleigh-riding down large swells off the port stern quarter. Fitz and I huddled in the cockpit against the chill air of the Gulf of Maine. We had the watch from 0400 to 0800 while our shipmates—my wife's cousin Dicken Crane, and her brother, Coe Kittredge—were snug in their bunks below. Only the presence of a nearly full moon and the promise of a very early sunrise—it was only two days after the summer solstice—afforded us some psychogenic warmth. It would be another day before our wonderful magic carpet, the 40-foot wooden sloop *Consolation,* would transport us around West Quoddy Head, Maine. There at the top of Maine and the end of the United States we would begin a waterborne summer adventure along the coast and among the islands of Maine.

A bright moon and an early sunrise are not the only things which warm the soul on a cold night's ocean passage. There is, too, the heightened intimacy generated by sharing a night watch on the high seas.

My shipmate, Cornelius "Fitz" Fitzpatrick, and I were not exactly birds of a feather. A large, barrel-chested man with a salt and pepper beard long enough to cover the second button on his shirt, Fitz is the mechanic at Brown Oil in Dalton, Massachusetts, in charge of all their trucks. But to call Fitz a grease monkey would be like calling Jascha Heifetz a fiddler or Toscanini a band leader. What Fitz doesn't know about a diesel engine would fit in the gap of a spark plug. Come to think of it, I don't believe diesel engines *have* spark plugs, which shows you how much I know.

While Fitz has been keeping Brown Oil's trucks rolling through frigid Berkshire County winters, I have spent the last twenty years working as a free-lance photographer for magazines such as *People* and *Time.* Because of my profession, doors have been opened for me beyond my wildest childhood dreams (I was a small boy when I first fantasized about becoming a photographer), but don't ever ask me to repair a Nikon or a Hasselblad . . . or a diesel engine.

As the first hint of dawn appeared off the starboard bow, Fitz and I tried to keep as warm as we could. My sleeping brother-in-law Coe, whose watch would not begin for another hour, had thought to bring along a pair of woolen gloves, a

Our wonderful magic carpet, the 40-foot wooden sloop *Consolation*.

piece of gear one does not necessarily expect would be necessary for a June passage across the Gulf of Maine. We were grateful, though, and traded them each time we alternated steering.

The long hours of the watch stimulate all sorts of conversation. At first one jokes and banters to stay awake. Toward the end of the watch, fatigue has the additional effect of reducing inhibitions; the talk becomes more personal. We spoke of my plans for the summer ahead. Soon, in Eastport, we would meet my wife Betsy, a lifelong sailor and fearless crew member, and nine-year-old daughter, Eliza, still a sea pup, albeit an enthusiastic one. We would begin the cruise I've dreamed of. For the next two and a half months Dicken, Eliza, Betsy, and I would range the coast of Maine, living aboard *Consolation.*

Fitz lamented the fact that he would not be aboard all summer. "You know," he said a little wistfully, "I'd be doing this in a flash if I could afford to." (Coe and Fitz, who were helping deliver *Consolation* from her winter home in Essex, Connecticut, to Eastport for the fun of it, would return to real life in a few days.)

I in turn fretted out loud about what seemed like a high potential for claustrophobia. We would be in tight quarters: four people on a 40-foot sailboat for eighty days. I suppose crew members on the *Niña, Pinta,* or *Santa María* would not be sympathetic, but it is a subject of great concern to the modern sailor. Alone among the four of us, I had crossed the Atlantic by sailboat. I had also sailed the four thousand plus miles from Hawaii to New Guinea, which—take it from me—is a long bloody way to sail. Dicken and his father Fred Crane, who owns *Consolation,* attempted a trans-Atlantic passage in 1987. They were stymied (and dreadfully disappointed) when a leak in the stuffing box forced them to turn back three weeks out. From these trips Dicken and I knew the special discipline it takes to maintain harmony in the close quarters of a sailboat. Each of us would need to pay scrupulous attention to manners, our sense of one another's space, and respect for private moments. There would be little enough room for the four of us and none whatsoever for thoughtlessness.

"Don't worry," Fitz reassured me, "you're going to have a super time. Super crew, super place. How can you miss?"

As I thought about it, what Fitz said made sense. How *could* we miss? I felt the fool for doubting.

The light of the moon gradually succumbed to the stronger predawn glow. The sky to the east was pink—not the reddish tone of the sailor's ditty "red sky in morning/sailor take warning," but the delicate color of a soft-hued, luminous rose quartz. I was settled back with my head on a cushion, which in turn was propped against the big winch we use for the genoa jib, finally feeling not a mite worried about anything. Even the chill seemed to be abating, although I still wore a heavy Irish sweater and a full set of foul weather gear on top of that. Manning the wheel, Fitz rocked gently from side to side with the steady movement of the boat. He kept a weather eye on the compass as he made minor course corrections. I once sailed with a guy who so oversteered that the sailboat's wake looked like a giant snake slithering behind us. Fitz's wake was arrow-straight. From time to time I

Intrepid passage-mates, *left to right*: Coe Kittredge, Dicken Crane, and "Fitz" Fitzpatrick.

could see him aligning a still visible star in the crook of where the spreader meets the mast. He would steer by that star for a while to relieve the monotony.

To the east of us against a spectacular pink tableau I watched flights of well-named greater shearwaters, their wing tips skimming mere millimeters from the surface. They never actually touched. I must, I thought, find out if their stiff-winged gliding technique is used for the pursuit of prey or for some other reason (like the sheer enjoyment of it?). Without being overly anthropomorphic, I could not help but think that their antics looked—at least to this earth-bound soul—like a great deal of fun.

The seabirds accompanied us night and day as fellow travelers. They were the only creatures we saw out of sight of land except the occasional herd of porpoises skittering about the bow. Earlier, while it was still dark, the storm petrels had swooped and darted above *Consolation*'s stern like old friends keeping us company during the chilly night watch.

I asked Fitz if he would like a cup of coffee to ease him into the new day. As I

***Consolation*, in all her glory, bounds across the Gulf of Maine.**

went down the companionway I heard Fitz say, "Sugar, no milk, please." In *Consolation*'s compact saloon I flicked the switch on the circuit breaker board marked Propane and lit a burner on top of the range. I filled the aged coffee percolator—the kind with a center tube and a perforated aluminum basket at the top for the coffee grounds—and set it on the fire. While I waited, I glanced around the small saloon that was to be our home away from home.

Happily curled up in one of the bunks, my brother-in-law Coe snored away the rest of his off-watch time. As I looked at him, I was reminded of what a pleasure he is to sail with. He loves sailing—more than anything, perhaps—and it would never occur to him not to chip in and do more than his share of "ship's work."

Indeed, my thirty-six-year-old brother-in-law deserves nothing but admiration for all his stellar qualities—save his snoring. Coe, you see, snores louder than one would think humanly possible. Betsy, my sainted wife, claims that I snore, too, but I have heard no evidence of that myself. She likes to quote Tom Sawyer on the subject: "There ain't no way to find out why a snorer can't hear himself snore."

The coffee finally started to perc. Balancing two cups, I climbed the ladder back to the cockpit, where Fitz, the helm between his two gloved hands, steered NE by E—down east across the Gulf of Maine.

Finally, at 0800, two sleepy heads emerged from the saloon. Dicken was brushing his teeth. "Hope it's not too cold up there," he said with a foamy grin. "I've just taken the sweaters off my teeth."

On that happy note, Fitz and I were officially relieved, and we went below. I stripped off my foul weather gear, sweater, long johns, and climbed gratefully into my berth in the forward cabin. If we were lucky, I thought sleepily, we would be in Maine tomorrow.

Contented with my crewmates—friends—and looking forward to being reunited with Betsy and Eliza in Eastport, I was asleep almost instantly.

One
QUODDY TIDES

Our destination: The lighthouse at West Quoddy Head, Maine, on the easternmost point of land in the United States.

I NEARLY MISSED HER AT FIRST, she looked so small in the field of view of *Consolation*'s powerful binoculars. But Eliza's sharp nine-year-old eyes had spotted us well before, and she was waving furiously. Then I saw Betsy emerge from her harbor-side motel room through a sliding glass door. She was wearing only a towel, her morning shower having been interrupted. I got the familiar lump in my throat that I do after even a short separation and waved back just as furiously.

Betsy and Eliza had driven to Maine to meet us at the end of our sixty-hour, 392-mile down east passage. And in one of those logistical maneuvers made necessary by the nature of cruising, my wife and daughter would trade places with Fitz and Coe, who would in turn drive the car home.

The fuel dock where we tied up was a stone's throw from The Motel East, the advertising slogan of which no doubt accurately extolled its virtues: Quiet, Quality. As we made *Consolation* fast, I jumped onto the float and immediately experienced the curious effect of "land legs": the mild dizziness, disorientation, and rubber knees one gets after being at sea for five days. But the real dizziness came from looking up the rickety ladder, which reached three stories from the float at low tide up to the top of the long-legged dock. It was a reminder of the extreme tidal ranges that occur down east.

The day we arrived in Passamaquoddy Bay, one day before the full moon, the range of the spring tide was over twenty-one feet. This is not as sensational as the fifty-three-foot rise a hundred miles farther northeast in the upper reaches of the Bay of Fundy, which has the highest tidal range in the world. But it is enough to discourage many a cruising yachtsman from venturing as far down east as Eastport.

Compare, if you will, a twenty-one-foot Eastport tide to a seven-foot tide in New York Harbor or the one- to two-foot tidal range in Miami. The difference is dramatic and has profound implications for the visiting sailor. At Eastport's rate, the tide is rising or falling three-quarters of an inch a minute, and seventy billion cubic feet of water race in and out of Passamaquoddy Bay every six hours, which is more water than flows down the Mississippi in two weeks.

So it was with a mixture of horror and delight that I saw Eliza negotiating the incredibly long ladder to greet her dad on the float below.

We hugged and kissed, and she was full of reports of their twelve-hour drive up to Eastport. Having hastily dressed, Betsy descended next, inching down the treacherous ladder—slippery for being submerged half the time. When she was safely on aboard *Consolation,* we also hugged and kissed. Eliza greeted her Uncle Coe and her pals, Dicken and Fitz.

It was a happy reunion for all. But there was work to do.

The first landfall after five days is the time to reprovision. Betsy, my wife of twelve years, had stopped on her way up and filled the trunk of our eight-year-old Saab with food and liquor (the latter, from one of those inexpensive New Hampshire State Liquor supermarkets located with their own exit ramps off I-95). Betsy is incredibly good at the logistical challenges of provisioning, just as she would be invaluable aboard *Consolation* in her role as navigator—guiding us through cuts, avoiding rocks and shoals, and getting us from port to port in one piece. But you would not think of Betsy as the organized type on first meeting. She has a wild mane of wavy/curly blond hair, which, unless it's gathered up, gives her the appearance of a latter-day earth mother. She once told me that when she was a teenager her hair so embarrassed her that she tried to iron it straight. Now, actresses and models say to her, oh, I so envy your hair, how do you do it? Her personality is one of a straight shooter; she minces no words, brooks no hypocrisy.

The waterfront at Eastport where a twenty-one-foot spring tidal range is the rule.

At the same time, people, sometimes complete strangers, hasten to confide in her. I sometimes think they line up at her kitchen door as if it's a church confessional. Whatever the bewitching ingredient, people just plain like her. I do, too. For me it is especially convenient that my best friend and the woman I love are the same person.

Betsy handed out the *petits commissions:* Eliza, Fitz, and I were dispatched to S. L. Wadsworth & Son's Hardware, Paint & Marine Supplies for half a dozen perennial shipboard necessities like batteries, shock cord, and marline; Coe was placed in charge of beer; and Dicken and Betsy would tackle the A & P to replenish fresh vegetables, dairy, and meat stuffs.

After paying for our purchases, we continued "uptown." Along the way I picked up a copy of the local paper, *The Quoddy Tides,* which is edited and published "on the 2nd and 4th Fridays of each month" by Mrs. Winifred French. The logo of the paper included the line drawing of a lighthouse, a schooner, and a fishing boat and the subhead: "Most Easterly Newspaper Published in the United States." One would be hard-pressed to require news of the Eastport/Lubec area *not* covered by *The Quoddy Tides.* With regular features such as "Book Nook by Bea," "Outdoors with Ed," "What's Cookin'," and a letters-to-the-editor department named with Eastport's interdependence with the sea in mind: "Mail Boat Rex IV," what more could one want? One small box in the "Whirlpool" section especially caught my attention; it described early summer on Passamaquoddy Bay: "Lilac time—and also lupines brightening fields and some gardens; brilliant large orange oriental poppies opening up on the south side of many gardens; grass has had to be cut on lawns a number of times already; leaves on trees are fully out now—it is June in the Quoddy Bay area."

Loading our various provisions was a production made more complicated by those wicked tides. Complicated is not the right word; actually, the system was simple, but slow. There is a small derrick, a rope, a pulley, and a basket. You lower each bag of groceries hand over hand, one bag at a time down to your helper on the deck far below while another helper stows the cans, boxes, and bottles wherever they fit in nooks and crannies throughout the boat. Thus finally reprovisioned we decided to head across to the Lubec side of Johnson Bay. We would anchor in the crotch of Lubec Neck with good protection, even though the wind and the sea were getting more boisterous. Doing so would save us a dockage fee for a night's stay as well as spare us the noise and commotion of Eastport's busy little twenty-four-hour harbor.

It is characteristic of the Maine coast that the quickest way to get from one harbor to another is more often than not by boat. *Consolation* can sail from Eastport to Lubec in twenty-five minutes; it is only three and a half miles away. If, however, you wish to drive to Lubec, the shortest road is forty miles long, and, if you decide to walk the serpentine shoreline, your trip would be more than a hundred miles long. Maine itself is enormous. Not only is it the largest state in New England, but it is bigger than the other five put together.

In no time at all we scooted across the bay. Dicken deftly executed an elegant

Eastport is the easternmost deep-water harbor in the United States—"makin' it a day closer to Europe."

Fulton's Cabins, Pembroke, Maine—"Heated, Showers, TV."

anchoring-under-sail maneuver. At just the right instant he steered *Consolation* into the wind so that she would lose her momentum at the precise spot where Coe could drop the anchor. None of that sissy drop-the-sails-and-turn-on-the-engine stuff for Dicken. In fact, there is not a sissy bone in Dicken's muscular body, nor, I hasten to add, is there a macho one. Soft spoken and omni-competent in everything nautical, Dicken would be captain of his father's boat for most of the summer. Betsy and I would share in the sailing and navigational duties, but I gladly ceded to Dicken the ultimate responsibility that only a captain can shoulder for his vessel. In this, no better choice could have been made.

For fifteen years Dicken Crane has logged the forests of his native Berkshire Mountains in western Massachusetts. Operating out of a post and beam cabin in the woods, which he built himself, Dicken bypassed the family business, Crane & Company, the papermakers in nearby Dalton, Massachusetts. Crane is the company from which his father Fred recently retired and for which his brother Tim does research and development. It was to the woods instead of the boardroom that Dicken was lured. During our summer together, I would learn much about the natural world from Dicken. His knowledge of geology, flora, and fauna is extensive, and he can explain natural complexities with a disarming simplicity. His ability, for example, to identify birds in flight is phenomenal. To walk with Dicken in the forest is like taking a cram course in botany, biology, ecology, and geology all together—only a lot more fun than doing so in school. Even the way he walks is telling. Fully erect, shoulders hardly bouncing with his rapid stride, he barely cracks a twig or brushes a branch. One is reminded of what must have been the motion of the prototypical eighteenth-century Native American Dicken so greatly admires.

Dicken's anchoring-under-sail trick had attracted the attention of two men who were working on the Sea Farm salmon pen in Johnson Bay. After we had settled at anchor, dropped and furled the mainsail, and sorted ourselves out, they powered over in a beaten-up outboard motorboat for a visit.

"Hello, there," one said as his companion effortlessly drew up beside us and cut his engine. "We saw you sail across Friar Roads. Pretty boat, you have. Real pretty."

"Well, thank you," I replied. I introduced our ample crew of six to the man standing in the bow. He was called Charlie Rier, a deeply tanned man with bushy brown hair. He was wearing a faded denim shirt with the arms cut off and looked like he had spent a lot of time outdoors. I shook hands with his buddy Mike and felt the calluses of a man who had obviously hauled a lot of line in his thirty-odd years.

"I was saying to Mike," Charlie continued, "when we saw your boat, 'We've got to get one of those!' "

"You should," Coe joined in.

"Can't really afford one," Charlie said perfectly cheerfully. Without missing a beat, he reached into a bucket and lifted out five freshly filleted Atlantic salmon. They looked at least five pounds each. "We were wondering, would you have any use for these?" Charlie asked. As a gift from an old friend, an offering of twenty-five pounds of salmon would have been overwhelming. From a perfect stranger it was mind-bogglingly generous. We fell over one another trying to produce a suitably appropriate response.

After a profusion of thank-yous from our gang, I offered them a beer.

"No thanks."

A Coca-Cola?

"No thanks."

"Would you like to come aboard? Look around?"

"Okay." A chance to look below seemed to be all they would accept in return for such a generous present.

If one had to conjure up an image of a Maine fisherman, words like *laconic, reserved,* even *standoffish* might enter the mind. Such stereotypes are perpetuated. John Steinbeck was given the following advice by a Mainer and wrote of it in *Travels with Charley:*

" 'Don't ever ask directions of a Maine native,' I was told.

" 'Why ever not?'

" 'Somehow we think it is funny to misdirect people and we don't smile when we do it, but we laugh inwardly. It is our nature.' "

Indeed, naysayers I spoke with in advance of the trip warned me to expect a certain aloofness (I think that is a polite way to put it) from the Mainers I might wish to photograph and write about. These two fishermen—the first of the many we would meet—completely quashed such an idiotic notion. I felt in some not quite rational way that we had been officially welcomed to Maine and that the summer seemed wonderfully promising.

***Consolation* at anchor in Johnson Bay near Lubec. One of the Sea Farm salmon pens is visible in the right background.**

Two

"HOGGIE" IS A FREIGHTER

In the end Charlie Rier and his friend Mike accepted soft drinks and told us of their work on the salmon pens. We sat in *Consolation*'s cockpit companionably, if a little cramped, sipping our sodas.

The business of aquaculture or fish farming, Charlie explained, is a relatively new one. The company he works for, Sea Farm, began as a joint Canadian-Norwegian venture and moved into the Cobscook-Passamaquoddy area because of the area's unique combination of hospitable features: the right water temperature, salinity, oxygen level. Most important, though, are the rapid currents caused by the huge tidal range, which serve to flush the bottom clear of detritus with each change of the tide—not unlike a giant toilet. Each pen holds six thousand Atlantic salmon, and there are twenty pens. Without the flushing action of the tides the water would soon be uninhabitable for such an enormous concentration of fish.

Summer, spring, fall, and winter, no matter the weather, two men must make their way out to the pens twice daily to feed the smolts their healthy mixture of herring meal and vitamins. This, at the worst of times, can be grueling work. The pens are surrounded by steel mesh walkways, which are only a few feet above sea level. I tried to imagine what it must be like out there during a January blizzard when it's "blowin' like stink" and when the workers have to struggle just to save themselves from being blown off the catwalk. A poke in the eye with a sharp stick strikes me as more appealing.

After two years of careful nurturing, the salmon are harvested, cleaned, iced, and shipped to Boston's Logan Airport as quickly as Sea Farm can get them there. They are transported in insulated cardboard boxes; the ice keeps them just a hair above freezing; and the top-graded salmon are of a quality to merit air-shipping them all over the world.

I asked Charlie Rier how Sea Farm was faring in the aquaculture business. Pointing across Johnson Bay to the twenty Sea Farm pens filled with leaping salmon, Charlie said with obvious pride, "Money machines." What he did not add was the astonishing fact that in 1992 fish farming would surpass for the first time the almighty Maine lobster industry in total revenue.

"Speaking of fish," said Charlie Rier flashing his friendly grin, "my uncle

For the first time, fish farming would surpass the almighty Maine lobster industry in total revenue.

Fattening up in twenty pens are 120,000 Atlantic salmon.

owns the Old Sardine Village Museum in Lubec. You must visit him. He's quite a character. Just tell him Charlie sent you. His name's Barney Rier." When Charlie said his uncle's name, it sounded to my ears like *Bonnie Eye-a.* The only man I could think of with the name Bonnie was Bonnie Prince Charlie, so I was sure I had gotten something wrong there. I asked him to spell the name, and it came out *Barney Rier.* Charlie laughed when I told him what I thought he'd said. "We don't pronounce the *r*'s hereabouts," he explained.

To the tune of much derisive laughter amongst *Consolation*'s crew, I admitted I would have to fine-tune my ear to the down east way of speaking. Just as a New Yorker can tag an out-of-towner for mispronouncing Houston Street (One mustn't think of Sam Houston, Father of Texas; it's pronounced *How'stun.*) a State-of-Mainer has you instantly and certainly pegged if you don't call Saco, Maine, *Socko;* if you don't know that Calais rhymes with *Alice;* or if you don't know that *Bonnie Eye-a* and Barney Rier are the same fellow.

My knowledge of sardines being limited to the fact that they are herring with their heads chopped off, I proposed we mount an afternoon expedition to Barney Rier's museum. All hands, save one, signed on with enthusiasm. Dicken decided to stay behind, opting for a quiet moment (they can be all too infrequent on a crowded sailboat). Apparently, he felt his knowledge of sardines was sufficient to handle any foreseeable sardine emergency.

After lunch, having said another profusion of thanks to Mike and Charlie for the salmon, we loaded into *Consolation*'s dinghy, *Hog Wild,* for the short trip ashore. With the Bay working up a bit of a chop, Fitz, Coe, Betsy, Eliza, and I gingerly chose our seats for balance and weight distribution. Eliza, being the lightest and the only one among us except Dicken who did not mind jumping knee-deep into the frigid water to pull us ashore, sat on the narrow bow seat. Coe sat alone on the second seat, the rowing position, Fitz and I balanced out the third, and Betsy offset Eliza in the stern. There's no end to what you can fit in *Hog Wild* (or *Hoggie* as she is known to her friends). As Fred Crane likes to say, "*Hoggie* is a freighter."

If *Hog Wild* and *Consolation,* for that matter, seem like unusual names for pleasure craft, there is method in the Cranes' madness. After the war, Fred Crane's father (Dicken's grandfather), known to one and all as "Pop," satisfied a lifelong dream and commissioned a yawl to be built to his own specifications. She was constructed by Mathiessen & Paulsen, a Danish shipyard in Schleswig-Holstein. By all accounts she was a beauty. He named her *Caution* after what must surely be the most aptly named warship of all time: the minesweeper called *Caution,* which saw Pop Crane safely through the war.

After many summers cruising the coast of Maine, Pop Crane died in 1978. He left his beloved yawl to his son Fred. Not long thereafter, Fred bought a dinghy from the Jarvis Newman yard in Southwest Harbor. It was Joyce Crane, Fred's wife, whose witty, quirky mind determined that if your yawl is called *Caution,* your tender must be *Hog Wild.*

(I've spotted some other sailboat-tender combinations whose names I like equally well. Among them: *Brilliant* and her dory, *Afterglow*, and *Secret* and her trusty dinghy, *Secret Service*.)

In spite of the charmed wartime service of the minesweeper *Caution*, the luck of the yacht *Caution* ran out ten years ago. While she was laid up for the winter, she burned to a skeleton in a tragic boatyard fire. The family and all who loved her were devastated.

Fred immediately set out to replace the irreplaceable *Caution*. His search took him as far as Everglades City, Florida. There he found a 40-foot sloop called *Miss Possum*. Although she was a sloop instead of a yawl, she bore such an uncanny resemblance to *Caution* that Fred bought her on the spot. Joyce suggested that in deference to *Caution* they name her *Consolation*.

Although less than twenty years old, *Consolation* had already had quite a history. She was designed in 1959 by the legendary sail-maker turned yacht designer, Ted Hood. Hood built a dozen boats similar to *Consolation* at the Tor International Shipyard in Japan in the early sixties. They became known as Tor 40s. Fred's Tor 40 has been known by a variety of names: *Islandia* (1963–1972), *Ma'm'selle* (1972–1975), *Departure* (1975–1979), *Miss Possum* (1979–1982). It can be difficult with a boat, which has had as many owners as *Consolation* has, to assemble a history of her comings and goings. Fred's best efforts include the following: *Departure*'s owners, Lloyd and Martha Davidson, sailed her for three years around the world. They abandoned the fo'c'sle as the master stateroom and used it solely to store their voluminous scuba gear, they were such avid divers. A man from Baltimore, Ed Hartman, sailed her not once but twice in the Capetown–Rio Race, a grueling 3,800-mile crossing intended for exceptionally seaworthy and usually much larger sailboats. Once Dicken was approached by a man at the Camden Yacht Club, who was, coincidentally, named Crane too. "I crewed on your boat," he told Dicken, "on a race from Capetown to Rio. I remember it blew so hard we suffered a knock-down. We put the spreaders in the water." (In landlubber's terms: She tipped over.)

Consolation has logged a prodigious number of sea miles and has had more adventures than we will ever know; so, too, I suppose has *Hog Wild*. But both have been safe and true for skipper and crew alike.

It was, therefore, with complete confidence that we overloaded the stalwart little freighter, *Hoggie*, to row ashore in a freshening chop to visit Charlie Rier's Uncle Barney and his Old Sardine Village Museum.

The road to Barney's house was steep and under repair. A road crew toiled in the hot but windy afternoon guarded by two women in hard hats holding Stop/Slow signs. One of them had stopped an empty yellow school bus. Written in large black letters down the side of the bus was a legend that would have seemed more in place in Alaska than Lubec: State of Maine—Unorganized Territories. We passed a beauty parlor that advertised itself as Susie's Beauty Nook—Walk-ins Welcome. It seemed to be busy and successful. A little farther along a man stood on a wooden ladder painting the front of his house yellow. Just as we passed, his friend pulled up in a pick-up truck and shouted out the open window, "You're getting better at that, Cecil, there's more paint on the house than there is on you!"

Consolation: **Her beauty would be our secret weapon.**

It was clear on first meeting that Barney and Becky Rier were welcoming people and that they operated the Old Sardine Village Museum as much for the fun of it as for making money. They were a couple in their late sixties, early seventies (I'm guessing) and displayed the demeanor of hardworking and contented folk. Barney was dressed in a blue-and-white checked shirt with red-and-white striped suspenders, worn blue jeans, leather sandals, and a white, crushable woven straw hat. The color of his beard was evenly divided between auburn and gray whiskers. Becky had her brown hair pulled back from her face and held with two hair clips; she wore gold framed glasses and a smidgen of pale lipstick.

Both Riers, Barney and Becky, took us on a tour of the museum, which is stuffed with everything that has anything to do with the capturing, cleaning, and canning of sardines.

Of equal interest to me, though, was the state of Lubec, Maine, today, about which Barney was just as well informed. Barney had grown up in Lubec. His present house, which is behind the museum, is within sight of the house he was raised in. His description of town life sixty years ago emphasized how much has changed. Barney can remember that when he was a child he would long for the arrivals of the large three-masted schooners, and Down Easters returning from foreign ports of call. It was his only glimpse of life beyond Lubec, but it was a peek at the world.

"I remember once when the *Rebecca Douglas* came in to Lubec to load up," he said. "Don't know where she was heading next . . . but, gosh, you should have seen her. She was a big three-master, a big, beautiful Down Easter. Her bowsprit stretched out way above and halfway across Water Street. I'll never forget the smell of the pine tar of her rigging, the musty, salty smell of her canvas all neatly harbor-furled. One of the mates invited me aboard—I couldn't have been more than nine or ten—and asked me if I wanted to see a Chinaman. I said, you bet! Course, I'd never seen one before. They took me down to the galley, and there, sure enough, was a Chinaman. He was the cook and had one long black braid down his back. It was quite a thrill for me."

We were standing by the side door of the Rier's sardine museum. I had gathered just from looking around Lubec that—Susie's Beauty Nook's apparent success notwithstanding—the town and probably most of Washington County

Hoggie, among friends.

were a depressed area in what I knew was an economically depressed state. It was certainly not news that by the end of the eighties and the beginning of the nineties a pervasive recession had hit Maine, like most of New England, hard.

We had learned from the museum that one of the biggest businesses historically in the Eastport-Lubec area was sardine canning. I asked Barney to tell us more. He scowled and explained that the canning industry, which employed most local workers, had all but collapsed. At the turn of the century, he said, there were sixty-nine sardine factories in Maine; eighteen of them were in Lubec alone. Today there are two packing plants left in Lubec, and neither one operates full-time. Overseas competition is one reason, overfishing is another. Even tastes have changed. There was a time when no factory worker's lunch box would be without a tin of sardines. Preferences have apparently shifted from the sardine to super-chunk peanut butter. Becky Rier visibly shuddered at the thought.

Barney Rier, Lubec native.

My Danish-born mother used to eat sardines all the time. I can remember her having an open-faced sardine sandwich for lunch—a smørrebrod—at least a couple of times a week. For whatever reason she has not had a sardine in years. (I must remember to ask her why.)

The Canadian herring industry, however, continues to thrive, Barney told us, but only because it is heavily subsidized by both the provincial and federal governments. Today, in down east Maine, a can of sardines is probably imported from Canada. And the currency used to purchase it is unfortunately more likely to be a food stamp than a dollar bill.

The woes of a former sardine canner, it turns out, are many, but we would not solve Lubec's economic problems that afternoon. After a pause Barney suddenly

Barney Rier's treasures are guarded by his cat.

Beyond the wildflower field, of which he is so proud, sits a fifty-three-foot lighthouse. "Doesn't have a name," Barney remarked, "but we always called it the spark plug."

brightened and, turning to the person who had never even heard of supply and demand, said, "Eliza, would you like to see the house I was born in? You can see it from my wildflower field. Come on!"

We followed Barney up the dusty drive toward his house, which is sited on the top of a hill. We passed a barn with an unlikely collection of, well, stuff (one hesitates to call another man's treasures junk). The gray, deeply weathered wood siding was covered with wagon wheels and rusted farm implements and engine parts. Incongruously, through the open barn doors we could see an antique silver Rolls Royce. Sitting next to one of the front wheels was a large orange cat who glared at us as we passed as if he were in charge of the shiny automobile.

A breathtaking sight awaited us at the top of the hill. Barney gestured proudly at his field of wildflowers. We looked out over a most magnificent and colorful variety of flowers: yellow and orange hawkweed, ox-eye daisies, red and white clover, eyebrights, yarrow, and St. Johnswort. Far below beyond the orange and yellow, the red and white of the wildflowers, and the green of the grass was the navy blue water of Lubec Channel.

"Look," Barney said to Eliza, "way over there, can you see that house? That was the house I was born in."

Barney picked up a flower and showed it to Eliza. "When I was a child, Eliza, about your age, I was taught to call this Indian Tobacco, and my Daddy told me that if I smoked this flower I would never smoke tobacco as an adult." Eliza assured him with the certainty only a nine-year-old can truly muster that she had no intention of smoking anything, neither flower nor cigarette, ever. Barney scratched his beard and, since he is also a man with a philosophical bent, said, "We-lll, that's very interesting because I never smoked this Indian Tobacco when I was a kid, but I never smoked tobacco either. So I guess there's no tellin'."

Three

"PIÈCE DE GÂTEAU!"

WE KNOW SO LITTLE ABOUT our own nation's geography. Indeed, most of us think of the coast of Maine as running in a north-south direction. This is not true. If you lay the straight edge of a course plotter on a chart of the Maine coast with one end touching Kittery Point adjacent to the New Hampshire border and the other end at West Quoddy Head Lighthouse, you would discover why Mainers refer to going up the coast as heading east. In true degrees the direction from Kittery to Quoddy is 57° or NE by E, which is demonstrably more easterly than it is northerly.

The expression, *down east,* came from the early days of coastal sailing. Thundering up the coast, driven by the prevailing westerlies, propelled by acres of canvas, those exquisite clippers of commerce were sailing "down-wind toward the East . . . or down east."

To confuse matters further, when most folks "from away" use the term down east, they mean it as a synonym for the entire State of Maine. Maybe the merchants in Freeport, the gallery owners in Ogunquit, or the travel agents in Portland would wish you to think that, but nothing could be farther from the truth. In fact, most Mainers reserve down east to mean the easternmost third of the coast—roughly the section from Schoodic Point to Eastport.

The Schoodic Peninsula is in fact an important punctuation point separating two altogether different parts of the Maine coast. West of Schoodic are shopping malls crowded with out-of-state license plates, snazzy yacht clubs whose members wear tomato-colored trousers, and marinas, which have a ships' chandlery instead of a good-smelling back room filled with marline and tackle. East of Schoodic are daunting tides, some of the thickest fogs in the world, frigid waters, and awesome currents. The legend had it that if you continued east of Schoodic you would drop off the edge of the earth, which is what Columbus's crew expected would happen to them.

To the west is civilization. To the east are stretches of uninhabited coast and isolated fishing villages; a cornucopia of sea, bird, and animal life; pink and white granite shores; and, everywhere, the stakes of countless fishing weirs silhouetted against a shimmering sea.

As Messrs. Duncan and Ware put it in *A Cruising Guide to the New England Coast,* a book, which has assumed near biblical stature among cruising yachtsmen:

"To be headed east by Schoodic whistle before a summer sou'wester with Mt. Desert fading astern and the lonely spike of Petit Manon Light just visible on the port bow is about as close to perfection as a man can expect to come on this imperfect earth."

Sailing east of Schoodic is neither for the fainthearted nor the inexperienced, however. It is for the sailor who has the temperament to abandon itinerary, the freedom to sail where wind and tide permit, and the time to outwait the severest of fogs. Unfortunately for them, most yachtsmen cruising the coast of Maine have neither the wherewithal nor the inclination to make this commitment. Consequently, most of what you will be leaving astern if you sail east of Schoodic Point are other sailboats.

At the beginning of our summer in Maine, *Consolation* was sailing in the opposite direction—from east to west—and thus we were already fortunate enough to be in that isolated paradise called "down east."

Federal Harbor in Cobscook Bay, nine miles sail from Lubec, was about as close to the perfection Duncan and Ware were writing about as I could imagine. Sailing the nine miles from Lubec, we passed nary a pleasure boat getting to Federal—lobstermen, draggers, working boats, to be sure, but not one sailboat. I

Federal Harbor: There, I breathed deeply of the silence.

thought, as we passed uninhabited Red Island along the way, that we had found the isolation for which this part of the world is famous.

Federal is a cozy little harbor formed by four rocky headlands, one each on Hog Island, Long Island, Black Head, and Horan Head. We dropped the anchor just as the sun was slipping behind stands of balsam, spruce, and what Thoreau called "the tall arrowy white pines" in this most fabulous corner of the Pine Tree State. It was the hour of the day photographers refer to as golden time, when the color temperature of the light from the setting sun is so warm that it turns everything that is white—like *Consolation*'s hull—to gold. After the splash of the anchor, there was complete silence. We were alone. It was impossible to tell by looking and listening how far we were from civilization, but here for a short time we could perceive no evidence of the intrusive presence of a world peopled by man. Moments like this are rare in a bustling urban life such as the one I lead. I waited until everyone else went below to mix drinks and start preparations for the evening meal. (Two of Charlie Rier's salmon were on the menu.) When I was alone on deck, I walked quietly forward to the bow.

There, I breathed deeply of the silence.

A weak dawn light filtered through the two portholes and the translucent hatch in the forward cabin. The silence had been a pleasure to sleep in, and I awoke rested even though my watch said it was only a little past five. The water in the harbor was so still that from my bunk I could not even hear the familiar sound of it lapping against *Consolation*'s hull. I slipped out of my bunk, careful not to waken any of my comatose colleagues. As I threaded my way through the maze of bunks, sneakers, and socks—we were still six aboard—Captain Dicken, characteristically alone among the five, raised a lid and said, "Mornin', Chris."

We went up on deck into a fine sprinkle, more mist than drizzle. It felt good on my naked body. Chilly enough to wake you up, but not too cold to cause discomfort. Dicken once again astonished me by diving into water which could only be described as peter-shrinking. I watched Dicken splash and gasp in the frigid water. He had some liquid soap with him, and I think he broke the world's record for the fastest shampoo and rinse. He was back on deck in a flash, toweling himself off in the light rain.

With a steaming mug of coffee in hand and drizzle misting my eyeglasses, I sat in the cockpit and surveyed the water's edge in Federal Harbor. It was dead low tide, and I could see the full band of shore that exists between the tide lines. In effect this horizontal strip—known as the intertidal zone—belongs neither to the land nor to the sea. It is the product of the eternal semidiurnal rhythm of the tides. And the length of time that a particular strip of shore is uncovered by the receding water determines what can live and grow there.

Armed with my *Field Guide to the Atlantic Seashore,* a waterproof camera (Nikonos), and my trusty, if slightly beaten-up, Leitz tripod, I rowed ashore in *Hoggie* for a closer look.

Under the influence of the great tides of the Bay of Fundy, the intertidal zone along the shores of Federal Harbor is so broad that it makes it easier to

The intertidal zone. Long Island, Cobscook Bay.

identify the six different colored bands that comprise the zone. Here, where enormous tides and a rocky coastline come together, the flora and fauna, which live in the twenty or so vertical feet between flood tide and ebb, are exceptionally accessible.

First there is the black zone, which is actually *above* the high-water mark. It is truly where land meets sea. It appears to be devoid of life because we are so unaccustomed to seeing living things that are really black. But it is in fact a stripe of densely packed microscopic plant life, which is kept moist by the spray of crashing waves. Lichen and algae live here, forming a slick film over the rocks, which you know is treacherous if you have ever tried to climb out of a dinghy onto it.

The black zone, which occurs wherever high tide touches a rock, a piece of coral, or a man-made breakwater anywhere in the world, lies just above the periwinkle zone.

Periwinkles, which are vegetarian snails that eat the microorganisms of the black zone, live on the next lower band. They do so by scraping the rocks with a weird organ in the shape of a tightly wound continuous ribbon called the *radula.*

Made of the same horny substance that forms the hard outer covering of insects and lobsters—chitin—the radula in the common periwinkle has approximately 3,500 teeth. Presumably having so many teeth can be pretty handy if you're crunching rock all day.

Periwinkles are one of those creatures which are betwixt and between, evolutionarily speaking. As a species they are midway between beginning to leave the sea and becoming exclusively terrestrial. Consequently, the periwinkle lives at a level of the intertidal zone, which is only underwater during the twice-monthly spring tides.

I had always thought that spring tides got their name because they occurred in the spring, but I have since learned this is not so. Twice a month after the full and the new moon the tide rises higher and ebbs lower than during the rest of the month. This occurs when the sun and moon are in conjunction or in opposition (a day or so after a new moon or a full moon). The word *spring* derives from the Anglo-Saxon *springan,* "to move quickly." If you have ever seen an incoming spring tide rising against a Passamaquoddy jetty, you will appreciate the aptness of this term.

The neap tide, by the way, is the opposite. It is when the difference between the tides is least. Etymologists believe the word *neap* derives from the Norwegian *næpen* or "scarcely touching." Scarcely touching, it occurs to me, is an awfully nice way to think of a neap tide.

I continued investigating the intertidal zone, slipping and sliding on the barnacle zone, which is the next layer below the periwinkles. I had one leg of my tripod extended and was using it as an old man uses a cane: to keep from falling down. Fifty yards offshore aboard *Consolation,* everyone was now up and busy. Betsy and Eliza sat on the foredeck painting watercolors; both are avid painters. Coe and Fitz were giving the engine of *Hoggie*'s small outboard a tune-up. Called a Cruise 'n Carry—and inexplicably referred to by everyone aboard as Cash 'n Carry—its chief features are that it is amazingly light and surprisingly powerful. Its failing is that it is so noisy no one ever wants to use it. Why they were working on it baffled me; maybe Fitz missed repairing Brown Oil's trucks.

The rock barnacles are kings of the upper high-tide zone. They give this layer its distinctive grayish coloration. On any of Maine's rocky shores you will see trillions of them. Members of the arthropod family like crabs and lobsters (but the only member that lives a fixed and sedentary life), barnacles secrete the rock-hard shells in which they reside. When the tidal waters return to cover them over, the homely barnacle opens four interlocked plates, which resemble the doors of a missile silo. Out from this opening comes a feathered plume which flicks in and out like a snake's tongue, thus capturing the waterborne microorganisms the barnacle depends upon for nourishment.

The lower three strata of the intertidal zone are covered with water from half to most of the time; they are in descending order the rockweed, the Irish moss, and the laminarian zones. These layers contain a dancing submarine forest. The first is inhabited by the purplish-brown seaweeds known as rockweed or wrack. Bladder and spiral wracks, for example, have those small, paired air bladders into which the weed secretes a gas; they act like buoys to float the upper fronds of the plant when the tide moves in.

The rockweed and below it the undergrowth of Irish moss with its flat, spiky fronds provide shelter and sanctuary for a plethora of small creatures. At low tide those creatures too small to fight the surge of surf and tide find refuge in this jungle; so too do those sea creatures that need protection from sun and drying air as well as from land and airborne predators. At high tide the jungle is populated by snails, crabs, and small fish darting among the swaying fronds.

At the very bottom of the intertidal zone uncovered only during the lowest ebb of a spring tide is the laminarian zone, home of the brown algae—the kelps,

Watercolorists on the foredeck.

winged and horsetail, the oarweeds and the devil's aprons. With long, dark ribbon-like fronds the laminarians stream out with the pull of the tide. Some, like the sugar kelp, have fronds which can grow as long as thirty feet.

Heavily populating the lower zones as if they comprised the underwater equivalent of greater metropolitan areas are the ubiquitous blue-black mussels. Clinging so tenaciously to whatever foothold they have been able to stake for themselves, colonies of mussels are packed so densely that they make sardine tins seem capacious.

On this particular drizzly morning at the lowest low of a spring tide the day after a full moon, I could photograph all these myriad elements of the intertidal zone—and then some. In atmospheric conditions such as these—a heavy overcast to diffuse the sunlight and a thin film of moisture to give everything a glossy radiance—colors can be deeply saturated almost to a surreal degree. The granite headland of Long Island, for instance, was an unbelievable shade of blue flecked with gray. Parts of it, when the light hit it right, were a rich indigo. Covering part of the rockweed layer was a stringy, slimy seaweed that looked like an enormous finely woven web but for its color. It had the chroma of what must have been pure chlorophyll. No product of nature, you would have thought, could possibly have such a hue. I can only describe it as chartreuse, but if that sounds ugly to you then I am not describing it well enough. It was, in fact, indescribably beautiful. Nearby, in a spectacular chromatic counterpoint, an orange and yellow starfish was awaiting the return of the high tide in a shallow tidal pool. And everywhere were the more mundanely hued black and blue mussels.

For those of us on a sailboat the ease with which mussels can be gathered is a pleasure. For such a delicacy to be so abundant always amazes me. Maine mussels are delicious, nutritious, simple to collect, painless to cook, and, best of all, free. Steam them in a little vermouth and garlic, wait until they open, save the broth to rinse them free of any residual grit, dip them in melted butter, and Yum! you've got an hors d'oeuvre every bit as good as one you can make from their harder-to-gather and tonier cousins, the clams.

Before returning to *Consolation,* I took the opportunity to fill *Hoggie*'s bailing bucket with mussels.

Lunch thus became a scrumptious combination of steamed mussels, drawn butter, and Betsy's sinful invention: the salmon sandwich.

North and east of us were the world-famous Cobscook Reversing Falls. They struck me as an emphatic *must* on my list of must-sees, particularly after I read this in Hank and Jan Taft's *A Cruising Guide to the Maine Coast:* "Cruising yachts are at substantial risk here . . . unless you have a great need for white-knuckle adventure, leave Whiting and Dennys bays for the eagles—or make the passage in someone else's boat."

And this in Duncan and Ware: "An equally experienced authority adds: 'I would discourage this. For anyone unaccustomed to these tides, it's fearsome.' "

There are approximately four square miles of water surface in Dennys and Whiting bays and heaven knows how many billions of gallons contained therein.

Four times daily—alternately draining and filling the bays—a good amount of this water passes through a three hundred-yard wide, one-half mile long passage between Leighton Neck and the north side of Falls Island; the rest flows through slightly-less-of-a-bottleneck between the south side of Falls Island and Race Point. Like the proverbial cork in the bottle, Falls Island sits in the middle creating Charybdian whirlpools, eddies, and a white-water rapids that *reverses* direction every six hours.

On the incoming tide, which apparently is the worse of the two, salt water flows over jutting rocks and ledges at speeds up to ten knots. The ledge just west of Falls Island, for instance, has a name with an ominous ring to it: Roaring Bull. During the middle two hours of the rising tide, when the greatest amount of water is surging through Cobscook Falls, the passage becomes a white-water river. And, if the wind and the tide are moving in opposite directions, standing waves can form between Falls Island and the mainland.

As the tidal current eases at slack water, the surface in still air becomes like glass. It is at this time—and only at this time—that a sailboat with an auxiliary engine can pass by Falls Island. Gradually, the current begins to flow back toward the Gulf of Maine; the rockweed is swept in the opposite direction; and small bubbles, twigs, and leaves gain speed across the surface. Following the very short interlude of slack water, the sound of the wind rustling the trees and the calling of wrens, warblers, and sparrows once again gives way to the roar of the water as the whole cycle is repeated.

There was no question whatsoever that we should match our seamanship against the reversing falls; the only question was whether to leave Falls Island to port (which the cruising guides suggested was the certain-death route) or to starboard (the merely-thumbing-one's-nose option).

Dicken, of course, voted for the "certain death" option, reasoning that, if *any* boatcrew could navigate the treacherous rapids of the Falls, *Consolation*'s could. Now, ordinarily a captain should not put matters that affect the safety of the vessel to a vote. It is almost a captain's job to be autocratic. But Dicken is not that kind of captain. When there is time to mull over two alternatives, Dicken, secure in himself, is content to be moved by the will of the group. In an emergency, however, he would not hesitate to issue orders.

As it often does, discretion conquered valor, and these six samurai opted for the less risky but by no means wimpy southern route between Ruth Point on Falls Island and Race Point on the mainland.

Timing was super-critical; indeed, the success of the adventure depended upon passing through the southern passage at high slack tide. We had been duly warned of dangerous unmarked ledges in addition to the turbulent currents, and passing through at the slack water at the end of the flood gave us our best crack at not cracking up.

When we reached Denbow Point, riding what we thought was the last of the flooding current, we dropped sails in order to negotiate the passage under power. We may have been brazen, but we were not going to be stupid. Coe went forward to look out for submerged rocks and ledges. Eliza assisted Coe, and Dicken steered. We passed Fox and Mink Islands, leaving them to port, and the current

Near the Cobscook Reversing Falls. From Dicken's log: "A low gossamer fog licked out from the land and wrapped around the ledges that low tide had left dark and looming."

was suddenly ebbing. As we headed for Huckins Island, the current flooded again. Around Ruth Point, it was ebbing, steadily. By the time we left Roaring Bull ledge safely in our wake the current had started to scream, but we were safely through. Dicken let out a loud hoot. Coe looked aft and let loose with a hearty, *"Pièce de gâteau!"* (which—I'm only guessing—must mean "piece of cake"). Fitz looked relieved. Only Eliza, the fearless one, expressed disappointment that it hadn't been scarier. Apparently, we had timed the transit perfectly, because, despite a few eddies and whirlpools, which Dicken handily traversed, the passage was an enormous anticlimax.

Now, all we had to do was wait six hours and retrace our steps as gracefully.

We busied ourselves with minor repairs while waiting for the hot afternoon to pass. Fitz tried to solve a persistent problem with the battery charging system, and Coe switched the back-up propane cylinder for the full one. We call this "ship's work," and all such activities are dutifully recorded by Dicken in *Consolation*'s log in hopes of currying favor with the owner.

When the work was finished, Fitz asked, "Did I ever tell you the one about the elderly couple from Maine?"

"His name was Wilbur George and hers was Alma," Fitz began the story, slipping into his best Maine accent. "Ayuh, Wilbur and Alma were on vacation, driving through South Carolina and stopped to fill up at an Esso station. While the pump jockey was cleaning their windshield, he asked, 'Where are you folks from?'

" 'Maine,' Wilbur replied.

"Alma, seated beside him on the front seat, demanded in her whining voice, 'What'd he say, Wilbur, you know I can't hear so good anymore?'

" 'Asked where we was from, Alma,' her husband repeated patiently.

" 'Say, what a coincidence, your being from Maine, I mean,' the pump jockey said. 'I was up in Lubec during the war, in the navy.'

" 'What'd he say?'

" 'Said he was down east during the war.'

" 'Come to think of it,' the pump jockey continued, 'I had the worst sexual experience of my life up in Maine.'

" 'What'd he say, Wilbur?'

" 'Said he thinks he knows ya.' "

I am an easy touch for Fitz's humor—his timing and mimicry are superb—and we had a good laugh at the expense of the hard-of-hearing Mrs. George.

Just then, Eliza poked her head above and asked if we could go ashore in *Hoggie* to view the north passage around Falls Island from Mahar Point. She was determined to see what all the fuss was about and whether those doomsday scenarios I had read aloud from the cruising guides had any merit. Sure enough, even from the safety of a State of Maine Scenic Overlook, the north passage looked like a rapids that could compete with one on the Colorado River. White water collided with rocks and ledges. There were vortices of swirling water that looked potent enough to set a 40-foot sloop spinning in a circle. Eliza looked up at me and said, succinctly: "No way, José!"

Before leaving, we ran into a local fellow named Bob MacAllister. By way of explaining how perilous the falls actually were, he told us the story of a old forester who logged Falls Island even though his wife had made him promise that he would not. The forester would use his dory to tow logs across the passage to Leighton Neck. One particularly rough winter day he fell overboard into the frigid water. He managed to grab one log under each arm, and, holding on for dear life, shot the rapids riding the logs to keep him afloat.

"They say he was exhausted, half-drowned, and three-quarters frozen when he came out the other side," MacAllister said. "Two fellows spotted him and waded in to haul him out. Although he was only partly conscious, he opened his eyes for a moment and grabbed one of them by the coat sleeve.

" 'For the love of God, man,' he implored, 'don't you ever tell my wife.' "

As departure time approached, a pair of dramatic anvil-topped thunderheads gathered overhead, and in their shade the temperature dropped palpably. We could hear the occasional rumbling of thunder to the west. The tide continued to ebb but at a slower rate. That was the cue for Fitz and Coe, whom Dicken calls the "anchor-yankers," to haul the anchor back on deck.

As we neared the precarious point of no return at the entrance to the passage, the heavens let loose in a deluge which reminded me of Gene Kelly's title dance in *Singing in the Rain.* In the pouring rain we fell over ourselves clambering down the companionway to the foul weather gear locker. It was crucial that we press through so as not to miss our brief window of opportunity. Coe and Fitz resumed a close watch on the foredeck. At low tide the rocks and ledges were that much more plentiful and dangerous. The lightning still flashed all around us, but to our dismay the impenetrable rain was replaced with a truly impenetrable fog, which, considering our position, was quite frightening. We kept silent so Dicken could hear Coe or Fitz's warnings from the bow: "Rock, Dicken, ROCK dead ahead." . . . "Go to the right, THE RIGHT! . . . Okay, steady as she goes." . . . "Watch out for the ledge on the port bow. . . . Slowly. . . . Okay, you're okay."

Dicken featured himself as quite *Consolation*'s Boswell and devoted a lot of energy to the ship's log. Let him describe our situation as we came up on a Falls Island we could no longer see: "The rain had passed leaving the hot rocks to steam. A low gossamer fog licked out from the land and wrapped around the ledges that low tide had left dark and looming. Now they wore white veils, when you could see them. As we followed the last of the ebb past Falls Island, there were several brief moments when everything disappeared . . . except fear."

On the next page Dicken added: "Once well in the narrows the warm land won over the cold water, and the fog was gone. The tide changed to flood by Denbow Island. Another thunderstorm just skimmed by us to the north. Lightning flashed dramatically in the east as we powered up into the Pennamaquan River. It was dusk when we anchored just before another squall came through. Things settled down for our late dinner of the best baked beans in the world."

As the thunder boomed and the lightning flashed, Coe and Fitz kept watch up forward. Fitz is apparently the more attractive of the two.

Four

THE BOLD COAST

WHAT IF MY HERO, that maestro of sentimentality, the film director, Frank Capra, had decided to set *It's a Wonderful Life* in a down east fishing village instead of in fictional Bedford Falls. He would have scouted up and down the coast looking for a suitably authentic location, and the moment he saw Cutler, Maine, he would have shouted, "Stop! This is it! Perfection!"

Cutler can *only* be described as picture perfect. I don't know if the town has ever been used as the backdrop for a movie, but it's certainly a dreamy setting for a still photograph. To that end I strolled up its main street carrying a camera bag hitched over one shoulder and a tripod balanced on the other. On porch after porch people sat rocking and chatting and admiring a view they must have seen all their lives—and clearly never tired of. Everyone I passed gave me a smile and a friendly nod or wave. It was early evening, and the colors in the sky were beginning to metamorphose into what promised to be a sensational sunset.

I was looking for a vantage point from which to make an overall photograph of Cutler's pristine jewel of a harbor when I heard a man's voice calling to me. "Come on up here on my lawn. I've got a fine view of the harbor. You can take a picture from here, if you'd like." I clambered up the steep lawn and introduced myself to an elderly gentleman.

"Name's Jay Potter Davis," he said quite formally, and we shook hands. He was a round-faced, slightly jowly man with ruddy cheeks, twinkly eyes, and he had the look of someone in the arms of a satisfying retirement. We chatted amiably, mostly about the stunning beauty of the evening.

"You know," he said, "I've lived in Cutler [he pronounced it *Cutlah*] all my life, and I watch people drive through town here all the time, people with out-of-state license plates. Most of them don't even stop. Can you believe it? Just speed right on through without hardly looking at one of the prettiest towns on the coast of Maine." Mr. Davis had made an observation that truly impressed me. I could imagine the owner of Ye Olde Gift Shoppe lamenting too few tourists, but for him, a lifelong resident, to feel that way was incomprehensibly generous.

After a minute or two of companionable silence during which I exposed a few frames of Kodachrome, I thanked Mr. Davis for his hospitality and bade him good evening. As I headed back down the hill, I heard him say, "That the boat you're off of, the pretty white one?"

I turned back to see him gesturing toward *Consolation* as she lay at anchor in the harbor below us. I answered, "Yes."

"She Fiberglas?"

"No, she's wood."

"Good," he said.

He said no more, but hearing the appreciation in his terse rejoinder gave me a warm feeling. I was proud of *Consolation,* and thought of her as my own. I worked hard to keep her spotless and fit—we all did—and it made a great deal of difference to me that a man such as he, who had spent his life with the sea, should admire her thus. I was starting to feel right at home in Cutler.

Jay Potter Davis: "They just speed right on through," he lamented, "without hardly looking at one of the prettiest towns on the coast of Maine."

The next morning I was eager to explore some more. It was a Sunday, and Eliza and I got an early start, leaving our companions to take advantage of "the day of rest."

Just as Falls Island sits like a cork in a bottle—an obstacle to the tidal flow into the great bays west of Cobscook—Little River Island lies smack between Eastern Knubble and Western Head defending the entrance to Cutler's peaceful harbor.

The harbor at Cutler: Quintessential down east Maine.

Behind an abandoned fishing weir—its herring-snaring days long over—lies Little River Island.

On the eastern side are three wharves constructed with elaborate underpinnings of crisscrossed logs, which at low tide, make them look as structurally complex as the Eiffel Tower. Bait shacks and fish houses perch on top of the wharves, which, of course, are built high enough to accommodate those wicked Fundy tides. Corbett's wharf, the northernmost of the three, supports the lobstermen's co-op and a shack with a driftwood sign with the name, Little River Lobster Co., painted on it. At high tide you can step conveniently from the top of these wharves into your skiff; at low tide you'd need a parachute.

There were only two sailboats in Cutler—three counting the new arrival. The rest were no-nonsense working boats, designed, built, and outfitted for Cutler's raison d'être: lobstering. Most of the lobster boats are named for wives and sweethearts: the *Sherry Lynn* and the *Debbie D,* for instance. Some are named with the whole family in mind (the *Five H*'s), and some are named with an eye to the long view *(Nick's Future).* My favorite was named by someone who evidently had respect for the sea; his boat was called *Fundy's Wrath.*

The old and new coexist in Cutler harbor. The balsam fir stakes of three fishing weirs (pronounced *wares,* hereabouts) rise forlornly from the depths of the harbor, abandoned and rotting, their herring-snaring days long over. Nearby an interlocked series of floating salmon pens are moored—the very picture of modernity with their circular floatation devices and bright green netting. Aquaculture has joined lobstering here. A state lobster hatchery opened in Cutler six years ago. There they nurture and raise larval lobsters in aerated tanks. By the time of their fifth molt when they reach an inch to an inch and a quarter in length, the lobsters are considered full-fledged bottom dwellers and are released into the waters around Cutler.

Across the harbor on Little River Island sits Little River Light, also forlorn because like so many other lighthouses in Maine its innards have been eviscerated, its windows boarded up, and its keeper replaced by a few wires and a computer chip. Gone is the throaty, deep-voiced sound of an old-fashioned foghorn; today the residents of Cutler listen to the annoyingly high-pitched dissonance of an electronic foghorn.

Eliza and I walked out onto Corbett's wharf, site of the Cutler lobstermen's co-op. It was empty this Sunday morning, because Maine law forbids lobstering on Sundays in the summer. We ventured into the bait shack, which was unlocked, and Eliza immediately rendered her opinion: "Yuk!" The foul odor of decomposing herring was overwhelming. Literally gagging, we lurched toward the door and fresh air and ran right smack into someone coming in.

A tall, thin man with suspenders grinned at our discomfort. "I'm Neil Corbett. How do you do?" he said. "Pretty gamy in there, isn't it?"

I introduced us, and we were again taken by the friendliness of the people of

Elaborate substructures are indispensable for spanning the extremes of Fundy tides.

Cutler. Mr. Corbett invited us to his house only a short distance from the wharf where, he told us, he had operated his lobster business for more than forty years. In his best years he had purchased over 250,000 pounds of lobsters each year from the lobstermen of Cutler.

Neil Corbett settled into an easy chair in his snug living room and without much prodding happily began to reminisce about a long, full life—a life about as foreign from Eliza's or my own as Nanook of the North's.

Neil Corbett's father was a lighthouse keeper. He first tended the big 178-foot light on Monhegan Island, then the now-abandoned lighthouse outside Tenants Harbor, and finally the Little River Light at Cutler. As Corbett spoke, my own mind briefly wandered back in time. As a schoolboy I had read the *Pickwick Papers,* and one line from the book popped out of the deep recesses of memory: " 'Anythin' for a quiet life,' as the man said when he took the situation at the lighthouse."

When the Coast Guard finally automated the Little River lighthouse, Neil's father had the sad distinction of being its last keeper. "I lived in that lighthouse for eighteen years," Neil Corbett recalled. "My father lived there even longer than that."

Little River Lighthouse, now automated, was home to Neil Corbett for eighteen years.

Neil Corbett.

The revolving light and the foghorn (which was actually a bell) were governed by mechanical clocks. "The clock revolved the light one complete turn every fifteen seconds," Neil said, "and if it was foggy the bell machine would hit the bell every thirty. When that clock came around to a certain point, it would trip a gizmo that would hit the bell."

The clocks were driven by a system of weights on chains like a grandfather clock. "Every five hours," he explained, "you'd have to wind those weights up just to keep the whole thing going, and it would run for six hours. Most generally, though, we'd wind 'em up again after about five. I used to come over to town at night, but I'd always plan on getting home in time to wind those weights if it was foggy. One July we had 525 hours of fog. Golly that was a lot of work!"

Corbett recalled bits and pieces of life on Little River Island, including this happily disjointed reminiscence of island husbandry: "We had a cow on Little River. We'd raise a pig or two, and we had hens and stuff like that. I never carried a flashlight. All the years that I was there I never carried a flashlight. I just got used to the dark. One night I come up over the hill and, by golly, right in the middle of the path that cow was laying there. Boy that took a jump on me, took a jump on her too! We lost a young cow once. We only had her a couple a weeks. She fell off the north side over there. She was feeding on the edge, eating the moss and such like and over she went. She hit the rocks and split her head right open. She was a nice cow, too, boy."

A hogshead barrel was a measure for fish. Here, used for a different purpose on Big Barred Island.

And he was proud of his memory of just being a boy: "I was one of those fellows who was always up to something. Always up to mischief, if you must know. I done something one time—I guess my brother and I got into a fight or something like that. My father says, 'All right, you're grounded. You're not going to get off this island for a week.'

"I jumped in the air at that. I says, 'I got off it didn't I?'

" 'Yeah, and that's as far as you're going.'

"Well about the third day I'd had enough. I said to my sister Ruth, I said, I think I know how I'm going to get off this island. I sawed an old hogshead barrel right in half, and I got into that tub. I hit the tide just right and by golly I went clear over to the other side and sculled her back again.

"My father, he heard about that, and didn't think much of it. But I done it just the same!"

Fourth of July was just around the corner. After we left the Corbetts, Eliza and I read a roster of events tacked to a bulletin board outside the Cutler General Store. It was a typed schedule, at the top of which was the imprint of a red lobster made with a rubber stamp. The rest said:

C U T L E R

4th of July Celebrations

July 4, Thursday

8:00 a.m. 7th Annual Cutler Harbor *5K ROAD RACE.* Contact Andrew Patterson for details.

9:00 a.m. CALLITHUMPIAN PARADE: fire trucks, floats, doll carriages, creped cycles, and horribles will assemble on the Crosman Wharf Road then parade to Grange.

10:00 a.m. FLAG RAISING CEREMONY: U.S. Navy Color Guard. Reading the military honor roll of Korean, Viet Nam, and Desert Storm Veterans. "Welcome Home Troops" essays by Christina Lemieux and Nicholas Bergeron. Pledge of Allegiance—National Anthem by SAD 77 Marching Band directed by Sandy Griswold.

10:30 a.m. CHILDREN'S GAMES: Soda guzzling, bubble gum contests, foot races, and penny scrambles for money prizes.

12:00 p.m. TURKEY DINNER: Sponsored by the United Methodist Women.

1:00 p.m. LOBSTER BOAT RACES: for cash prizes—Contact Brian Cates for details.

In case of rain: only the parade and children's games will be canceled. The Flag Raising Ceremony will be delayed until 11:00 a.m., and held in the Methodist Church, followed by the turkey dinner.

July 6, Saturday:

9:00 p.m. WELCOME HOME DANCE: Featuring Custom Made Country in the Grange upstairs, sponsored by the Cutler Volunteer Firemen.

It would be sad to miss what promised to be a fine Fourth of July, but we had already planned to be in Jonesport for the Fourth. I was especially disappointed that Eliza and I would miss the "horribles" in the Callithumpian Parade. Whatever the "horribles" were, they sounded heavenly.

Near the Lobster Hatchery, which shares a building with the Cutler Town Hall, is a crescent beach of mud and pebbles. There, Eliza and I came across the *Lacey J.* careened on the shore.

You cannot sail the down east coast without becoming enamored of that great symbol of Maine—the lobster boat. Elegant yet simple, the silhouette of these sturdy working boats is the heritage of generations of craftsmanship guided by an aesthetic sensibility no school of marine architecture teaches.

Gradually, I was becoming more adept at spotting the differences between different types of lobster boats. But I had much to learn before I could identify at a glance which yard or builder had built which boat, the way most lobstermen can.

The *Lacey J.* was already partly out of the water, and I could see that her lines were especially beautiful. Her owner, Wendell Bryant, was waiting for the tide to fall farther so he could work on her. His wife, Donna, and Rosie, their new Beagle puppy, were keeping him company that Sunday morning. Eliza instantly fell in love with Rosie and started some serious patting. But I was enamored of the *Lacey J.* Bryant had painted her hull an intense ultramarine blue and her topsides and shelter cabin, the palest shade of robin's egg blue. On her waterline he had painted a white stripe, which perfectly complemented her graceful sheer. Her bottom was exactly the shade of red a boat's underside should be. For a working boat she was in pristine condition, and I made a remark to that effect. Wendell Bryant accepted my compliment with a laconic "Ayuh." He added, rather sadly I thought, "Some people say I'm too fussy . . ." and let the thought hang. It occurred to me that what he meant was: *It would be impossible to put too much work into my baby.*

Separating Eliza and Rosie was an upsetting business, but eventually we started back toward the village center. We stopped to admire the white clapboard Methodist Church, which sits on a hill behind the middle wharf. From looking at it I noticed that Cutler—not unlike other small New England towns of the same age—must have run out of money at one point. The church has a flat-topped tower, which ends abruptly about a quarter of a story above the peak of the roof at a point no architect ever intended. Sadly absent is a steeple. About to be absent is the minister, who had just quit. I learned this from Jasper Cates, who was rummaging through a pile of old wooden traps looking for one to give the departing cleric as a souvenir of Maine. He was moving to North Carolina.

Jasper . . . Jasper Cates . . . the name sounded familiar to me. I felt sure I had seen the name somewhere, but where? Suddenly I remembered. I said, "Are you the same Jasper Cates, who is on the board of directors of the Maine Coast Heritage Trust?"

"Why yes," he replied with a pleased grin, "are you interested in what we're trying to do?"

Jasper Cates, director of the Maine Coast Heritage Trust, empties a truck-load of foul-smelling lobster bait.

I told him emphatically I was, and he suggested I come up to his house for a cup of coffee.

Having dropped Eliza back at the boat, I knocked on the door of the Cates house. From their porch one gets a terrific view of the harbor and Western Head beyond.

Jasper Cates has lived his whole life in Cutler. His ancestor, Robert Cates, was one of the four original settlers in 1785. He is a man, I quickly learned, of boundless energy. Both a lobsterman and the former first selectman of Cutler, he talks in machine gun bursts. The staccato urgency with which he explains complicated issues is magnified by a stutter. Some people who stutter sound like they are faltering over the word or thought. When Jasper Cates stutters, it sounds like the thoughts are coming too fast for the words.

He has, he told me, been a member of the board of the Maine Coast Heritage Trust for over half its twenty-year life. He proudly added that he was a big-time troublemaker as well. He described one land developer with whom he was doing battle as "having more faces than a totem pole." Mostly, though, he seemed happy to be on the barricades in such a crucial struggle.

"I got so much notoriety from that oil refinery flap over in Bucks Harbor, someone must've said, 'Get Jasper Cates because he's right in the thick of it.' Oh boy, was I ever in the thick of it. Sure was. We had meetings that ended up with people shaking their fists and hollerin', and some of them hated my guts. A few of them still do." His laughter, like his speech, is staccato. He continued, "Ha! Ha! Ha! I couldn't care less though, because I've got skin as thick as the battleship *Missouri.*"

The Maine Coast Heritage Trust was founded in 1970 through the leadership and financial support of Peggy (Mrs. David) Rockefeller, who lives on Mount Desert Island, and Thomas D. Cabot of Swans Island. A land conservancy organization with a strong preservationist bent, the Trust set out to save as many of the islands and special places along the coast as possible.

"The Bold Coast—I like to call it that—is unspoiled from Cross Island all the way to Quoddy Head," said Cates. "We realized we'd all have to get on the ball and keep it that way." Their original thrust was toward easements on the land. "We went along that route for quite a while and saved a lot of land, but then, by-and-by, we realized that we would have to buy land to save it."

Toward the end of the sixties before the formation of the Trust, there was a big push on to build an oil refinery near Machiasport at Bucks Harbor. Cates explained why and how he became an environmental and land conservancy proponent, and how he cut his activist teeth over this issue. As he saw it, his job was primarily one of public education. In an area as economically depressed as the Bold Coast, the prospect of a big industrial project such as an oil refinery sounded pretty good to most people.

Listen to Jasper Cates: "When they wanted to build the refinery, there were those that thought, Ah! the goose that's laid the golden egg. Our future's assured. We'll all get jobs. We'll get jobs building it. We'll get jobs working in it afterwards. And we've all died and gone to heaven. They didn't realize that the build-

ing of it and the running of it is highly technical. They found that out up in Canada when they built one there; the local people got a few of the minor jobs, but that's all. The main thing is that when it was all said and done the real jobs went to computer guys and white collar types from away."

And on the environmental front: "Plus there's always a danger of a horrendous oil spill. This is a tremendous fishing area up here. Always has been up here in the Bay of Fundy and the Gulf of Maine. We didn't feel that this was the place to take the chance on an oil spill. We realized that in this economy you've got to have oil and it has to be refined. But there are some places where you shouldn't refine it, because it would interfere with other resources. And this is no place for it."

The activists (with the unforeseen help of several frightening oil spills in the Atlantic) eventually quashed the Bucks Harbor oil refinery project as well as another $500 million one proposed for Eastport. And it led them to realize the need for an organization to fight the inevitable next battle.

It turned out that Jasper Cates's next battlefield could be seen from his front

Overleaf

An example of what Jasper Cates is trying to preserve: Cutler's harbor.

MACHIAS
LAMOINE, MAINE

porch: the 250 acres of Western Head across the harbor. The Patten Corporation, a New Hampshire developer which garnered unwanted national notoriety in a "60 Minutes" television piece, wanted to build thirty-two homes on the peninsula. Again Cates tried to explain to people that they would gain nothing, and lose a great deal, in the venture. But it was his articulation of *why* such a beautiful piece of land should be left as is that impressed me the most. "We figured," Cates said, "that for everybody's good—not just for ours—but for *everybody's* good, some of this land should be left the way it is. Not only for the sake of the natural and marine resources but also for the sake of future generations who might want to see a piece of coastline looking like it once did. Like I told so many people, I'd hate to be the one, some time in the future, to have my grandson come to me and say, 'What was it like, Grandpa, before they tore this place all to pieces? Why didn't you save some of it for us?' I'd hate to be the one to try and have to explain that off."

I thought of Henry David Thoreau's famous quote: "In wildness is the preservation of the world."

For a complicated variety of reasons, but led by the energy of one Jasper Cates, the activists again won the day. "We kept up a steady drumbeat," Cates said. And at just the right moment Peggy Rockefeller, like a guardian angel, came up with a million dollars, encouraged a friend, Baroness Anne M. Franchetti, to add a half a million, and the Trust bought Western Head, guaranteeing that it will remain unspoiled forever.

The victory, of course, thrilled Cates. He modestly observed, "It's kind of funny. The chance of me, a fisherman down in Cutler, Maine, hobnobbing with the likes of those two—they both stayed right here in this house, you know. But we have a common goal and a common cause. I guess when you get to know these people they respect you."

After thanking Cates for the coffee and the inspiration, I returned to the wharf where I had left *Hog Wild.* Along the way I passed a monument erected in celebration of Cutler's Bicentennial in 1985. It was dedicated to:

Those Who Fashioned Our Heritage
and
Those Who Shall Shape Our Future

I felt sure that I had just met a member of the latter group.

Five

"HOMARUS AMERICANUS"

MOST AMERICAN STATES and Canadian provinces wring double-duty out of their automobile license plates. Like millions of midget, mobile billboards, marker tags rove the country promoting attributes, both real and imagined, of the state which issued them.

Some crow about the state's largess, like Tennessee's the Volunteer State; some include cute, and occasionally puzzling, sobriquets like New Jersey's the Garden State; and some sport little pictures like the ear of corn on Nebraska's tag and the launch of the space shuttle *Challenger* on Florida's (which always struck me as an image Floridians would rather forget). And why the Department of Motor Vehicles in Harrisburg is so certain that I've Got a Friend in Pennsylvania, I'll never know.

Mainers, being of a practical bent, opted for the catch-all approach: Some wise commissioner in Augusta decided to adorn the state license plate with both the legend Vacationland (to tout tourism, the state's second biggest industry) and a red stencil of that emblem for Maine—the lobster.

When you think about it, the words *Maine* and *lobster* fit so naturally together that you would be hard pressed to find a lobster on a menu that did *not* say it came from Maine. Believe it or not, although Mainers landed 23.3 million pounds of lobster last year, not all lobsters are caught in U.S. waters. Even Canadian-caught lobsters sometimes end up on your plate bragging that they are from Maine. When, for instance, were you last tempted by an item on the menu called Live New Brunswick Lobster?

Betsy and I were rowing around Cutler Harbor late in the afternoon when we chanced upon a lobsterman in his early thirties named Mark McGuire. I noticed that McGuire's boat had no name. When I asked him why, he merely shrugged and said, "Never got around to it, I guess. Just didn't seem very important to me." To me that was astonishing, but I held my tongue. There was something unusual and interesting about a man who didn't care about what to most boat owners is such a fundamental ritual. Consider the names of other working boats along the coast—*Sleepless Nights, Me & Dad,* and even *Charged It.* These are all names that clearly reveal something important about the owner, something central to his way of life.

We chatted for a while longer as I tried to get the measure of the man. He seemed amiable enough, invited us aboard to prove it, and had a ready smile under his blond mustache. I asked the obvious questions and received patient replies. How long had he been fishing? Sixteen years, since high school graduation. Married? Yes. Kids? Two. Age? Thirty-four. And, again, why no name for the boat? Dunno.

That last non-answer nagged me. Curiosity made me want to find out more about a man who would leave his boat unbaptized. I began to think of ways to wrangle an invitation to go lobstering.

"Say," Mark asked, short-circuiting my scheming, "would you like to join me and my boy tomorrow morning? Go out fishing? Thing is, though, you'd have to get up pretty early."

It was *extremely* early the next morning when Betsy generously rowed me across Cutler Harbor to Mark's boat. I was dressed as I would have been for a night watch, but the early morning chill cut through my foul weather jacket anyway.

Mark and his son Mark Jr. who's known as Skipper and works from time to time as his father's sternman, were dressed as if they were heading for the North Pole. It made me wonder if I hadn't misjudged the weather. I asked Skipper, a friendly red-headed thirteen-year-old who, his father proudly told me, batted .800 in Little League, exactly what he had on.

"I've got on long underwear (tops and bottoms), pants, three shirts, two pairs of socks, and my Thinsulate boots, but I only wear this in the summer when I'm sure it'll be sunny!" He was also wearing slicker bottoms and a hat.

We powered out of the harbor toward the rising sun, past the new salmon pens, past Little River Light and Western Head, the jutting headland Jasper Cates and his friends had plucked from the jaws of the developers.

"Look!" called Mark over the steady throb of his 135-horsepower Ford diesel. He pointed toward a towering balsam fir. There, in all its majesty, a bald eagle took to the sky. It had classic features, a white head and a white tail, and an awesome wingspan—at least seven feet separated the tips of its outermost feathers. It circled high above the boat, gave us the eagle eye (I swear it looked annoyed at our early morning intrusion), and soared beyond the unspoiled crest of Western Head until we could no longer see it. We reached the first string of Mark's traps a little after 5:30 A.M. Distinctive turquoise stripes on each buoy distinguish Mark's from those of his colleagues. He lays them out in strings of ten to make it easier to remember those he has hauled and those he has not on a given morning. When you have two hundred lobster pots to haul, such strings can help you find them too.

Nosing up to the first of his buoys, Mark made a deft sweep with his gaff and snared the potwarp, the rope that connects his buoy to the trap under thirty fathoms of icy water. He dropped the gaff back into its accustomed slot on the gunwale. Then in a blur of adroit bustle he pointed the boat into the wind, throttled back to the precise hum needed to render it motionless, flicked the rope potwarp first around a block and then around a winch, and hauled his pot aboard.

"Homarus Americanus"

Mark McGuire, one of Maine's ten thousand licensed lobstermen, works hard to eke out a living.

The hydraulic winch is a noisy contraption called a Hydro Slave; it was built in Rockland. The trap itself is a rectangular wire mesh affair with a concrete bottom to keep it on the bottom. Inside, divided by rope netting, are two principal chambers, which Mark calls the "kitchen" and the "bedroom" ends. The unbelievably foul-smelling bait—partially decomposed herring—is suspended in a net bag at the kitchen end. When the pots are hauled, most lobsters are found trapped in the bedroom end. There are two features mandated by law: an "escape hatch," which allows little ones to escape, and another device designed to rot away, thus freeing the lobsters if the trap is ever accidentally separated from its buoy (a so-called "ghost trap").

The first trap came shooting out of the water so fast that I thought it would crash into the block, but at the right instant Mark cut the power to the winch, and the trap landed in a spray of water on the gunwale with hardly a thud. He accomplished all this in a matter of minutes, and it took only one or two more for him to sort the keepers from the shorts (the law requires him to measure the carapace of the lobsters he traps and return to the sea those that fall outside the current size restrictions—those that are too small *and* too big), rebait his trap, drop it overboard, and head for his next turquoise buoy. Meantime, Skipper was filling net bait bags with herring to replace those his father was emptying out of the traps. Like a well-rehearsed dance, the whole process seemed deceptively effortless.

It was not, of course. Lobstering is actually brutal, dangerous, risky work. Not as bad, perhaps, as it was when lobster boats were powered by sail and lobstermen had to haul hundreds of fathoms of potwarp by hand, but it is still a tough way to earn a buck. Mark made light of it, of course—as any Maine lobsterman would—when he said, "All a lobsterman needs is a weak mind and a strong back."

But he added, "I love it. I love it out here on the water. I wouldn't trade this life for anybody's."

At the risk of offending most of coastal Maine I have to say that I am not the biggest fan of *Homarus americanus* that ever sailed down east (Dicken won't even eat lobsters, and Fitz claims that in olden days these bottom-feeders were so unpopular they were only fed to prisoners). In his *Field Guide to the Atlantic Seashore,* Kenneth Gosner dryly remarked that "lobsters are cannibals and scavengers, rejecting really putrid fare, but not fastidious otherwise." Mark explained that the practice of banding lobsters's claws is not for the safety of the consumer but rather to prevent them from eating one another. And a friend of mine once observed: "I love lobsters, but, if you saw one in your basement crawling out from behind the furnace, *would you want to eat it?*"

Nevertheless, those "terrible cannibals," as Mark McGuire calls the source of his livelihood, are such a popular delicacy that they earn Maine lobstermen nearly $60 million annually.

At the end of the nineteenth century there were about two thousand lobstermen hauling a hundred thousand traps for a net yield of 22 million pounds. One hundred years later Maine issued ten thousand lobstering licenses. Those ten thousand lobstermen fished two *million* traps and caught 23.3 million pounds.

The day's catch is weighed, stored in a submerged crate, and Mark's account credited.

Many, many more lobstermen are competing for almost exactly the same yield.

Have you ever heard a farmer say, "I'll have a terrific harvest this year? Yup, this'll be my best year ever." Of course not, and lobstermen are the same way. They grouse about the waters being "all fished out," how low the price per pound is, and most of all about those damned state regulators, the "Gummint Fishcrats." A man can still make a fair living from lobstering, but, make no mistake, it will not be an easy living.

By 2:00 P.M. Mark had hauled 130 lobster pots, and Skipper had banded the claws of about 75 lobsters. Many more had been thrown back as well as scores of crabs, sea urchins, sea weeds, and fish. We headed back to the co-op where Mark's catch would be weighed and his account credited. It was the end of the working day for Mark and Skipper, and they both looked beat.

I considered pursuing the mystery of the boat with no name, but I was pretty tired too.

Heading home.

Thirteen-year-old Skipper McGuire (Mark, Jr.) bands a lobster's claw—not to protect the consumer's finger but to keep "those terrible cannibals" from eating each other.

I returned to *Consolation* to take a nap. I made it back just in time to say good-bye to our stalwart crewmates, Fitz and Coe. It was a sad moment when Dicken rowed them ashore in a *Hoggie* heavily-laden with duffel and sleeping bags.

For the rest of our adventure, Betsy, Eliza, Dicken, and I would go it alone: we four, a tiny nuclear unit snug within the confines of a 40-foot sloop at once isolated from and connected to one of the most magnificent coastlines in the world.

Life below decks for the remaining crew: Dicken makes a log entry; Betsy appears fatigued after a round of dishes; Eliza draws; and the author's laptop computer sits idle as the photographer makes the exposure.

Six

LITTLE BROTHER OF THE ARCTIC

Kik-kik-kik! Killer terns shrieked at us, swooping and darting above our heads. In spite of the sticks we had been given to hold defensively above our heads, red-billed arctic terns repeatedly strafed us like a squadron of Zeros over Pearl Harbor.

I thought briefly that I was trapped in an Alfred Hitchcock movie and wondered how wise we were to be landing on a lonely, treeless, lump of granite, Machias Seal Island, ten miles out to sea amid a colony of nesting arctic terns.

I had not yet had time to read the flyer from the Canadian Wildlife Service of Environment Canada, which a young naturalist had given us upon landing. (Machias Seal Island, incidentally, is territory disputed by the United States and Canada and has been claimed by the Canadians since 1832.) The flyer, I later read, contained the following *caveat:* "The adult terns are very devoted parents and attempt to drive away any potential enemy that intrudes on their nesting area. As they dive toward the intruder they emit a rapid series of calls that normally end in a piercing scream; although the dive most often comes short of the intruder, it is not unusual for it to end in a solid strike. It is for this reason that hatwear is recommended to the visitor." Thanks, Environment Canada.

There was only one thing to do: Run for it. Once we were out of the immediate nesting area of the terns they no longer viewed us as a threat. The birds lowered their voices and turned their attention back to the care of their chicks.

From a safe distance with a super-telephoto lens I was able to make some dramatic pictures of the terns. A plumpish couple in their early forties drifted over to where we were standing on the windswept bluff in the lee of the Machias Seal Lighthouse. The couple might have been fellow tourists but for the fact that they both had an expensive pair of Leitz binoculars around their necks.

"It's nice to see you're interested in the terns," the woman said. "Most people who come here only want to see the puffins." I looked around and saw she was right. All the people who had arrived by tour boat from Jonesport were waiting impatiently to be led to the blinds where they could photograph the puffins. (We happened to be the only sailboat that had ventured offshore that particular July morning.)

An arctic tern strafes visitors on Machias Seal Island.

We introduced ourselves to the couple I now suspected were anything but tourists. "I'm Evie Weinstein," she replied, "and this is my husband, Steve Kress."

It was a little like walking through Trafalgar Square and bumping into Queen Elizabeth and Prince Philip. From my reading I knew that I had just met the internationally known founder, superintendent, and all-around guru of the Puffin Project—Stephen W. Kress. And, in the couple, I had met the Masters and Johnson of nuptially-inclined seabirds.

Starting in 1969 Kress, a National Audubon research biologist and professor of ornithology at Cornell, began to imagine ways of restoring some species of

The Masters and Johnson of nuptially-inclined seabirds: Evie Weinstein and Steve Kress pose in the rain.

seabirds to their former colonial abundance along the coast of Maine. Kress chose Eastern Egg Rock—half the size of Machias Seal and twice as desolate—as the venue for the first experiment. He chose the Atlantic puffin as the experimental bird.

He could not have made a better choice. The almost unbearably cute puffin with its orange feet, multicolored beak, and doleful expression quickly became a winning symbol for Kress's efforts. The puffin's Latin name is *Fratercula arctica,* which means "little brother of the Arctic"; the French geographer Samuel de Champlain called this sad-eyed bird a "perroquet" or sea parrot. Either way, as Evie candidly told me, the puffin excels as a fundraising tool: "We are fortunate to have a bird like the puffin to attract the emotions of people to support this kind of work. What do you do if you're working with something like a snail darter? Or a bird that doesn't attract the attention of children and adults alike? We have some friends who are working with spiders. *I* think it's great, but good luck raising money."

Steve added, "Yes, there's something magical about a puffin for engaging the public. It's got everything going for it: A puffin stands vertically like people, it walks like people, it has bright colors, which people like, it doesn't have a hooked beak or hooked claws that might turn some people off. They're totally endearing and adorable."

Unfortunately for the puffin, its beguiling appearance almost caused its extinction. Toward the end of the nineteenth century, feathered hats had become the rage. To illustrate how prevalent they were at the time, the American Museum of Natural History ornithologist, Frank M. Chapman, conducted an informal survey along the New York City shopping street then known as Ladies' Mile. Of the 700 hats he passed in two afternoon walks, an astonishing 542 were crowned with birds' feathers. So many puffins and arctic terns (which were equally prized by milliners for their delicate plumage) were killed that by the turn of the century both species were virtually extirpated from the islands of Maine. In 1900 one nesting pair of puffins on Matinicus Rock was all that was left.

Enter Steve Kress three-quarters of a century later. He and a dedicated team of volunteers collected one-week-old puffin chicks—not much bigger than little puff balls—from sod burrows on Great Island, Newfoundland. One thousand miles away they relocated the nestlings to artificial burrows on Eastern Egg Rock, hand-fed them smelt and vitamin supplements three times a day, and crossed their fingers.

After an initial success on Eastern Egg Rock, Kress extended the Puffin Project to Seal Island in outer Penobscot Bay and then to Machias Seal Island where we now found ourselves. There are presently about nine hundred nesting pairs of puffins on Machias Seal. "This is very exciting," said Kress. "In the last hundred years the puffin has gone through an entire cycle from something that was a purely consumptive item to something that people will travel the whole length of the country to come to see and be *terribly* disappointed if they don't get a glimpse."

Fratercula arctica.

Using tape recorders and decoys, Kress also expanded the Puffin Project to include my friends, the arctic terns. "The concept is," he explained, "that you can actually initiate seabird colonies and have something to say about where they are going to choose to nest. You can't guarantee it, but you can stack the deck. You can attract seabirds with decoys and tape recordings and artificial burrows, whatever it takes to give the sound and ambiance of a colony. You can sell some of the birds, and, if you do it long enough, eventually it can click. It has worked spectacularly with the terns. We saw Seal Island increase from 15 pairs two years ago to 30 pairs last year to 650 pairs this year. We're very excited about this; it's probably our greatest success."

In spite of the aggressiveness with which they protected their nests from our "attack," the terns have a worse enemy than man, and it is the sea gull. Because we had arrived by sailboat, Evie Weinstein told us an anecdote about the eternal gull-tern war. The common herring gull, she said, who loves nothing more than devouring tern eggs and chicks, has a distinctive orange spot on its bill. That same orange spot represents to a tern what a red cape does to a bull: It is the unifying focus of a tern's animosity toward the sea gull. One day a sailboat sailed up to Machias Seal Island under spinnaker and mainsail. The spinnaker happened to have a large orange circle on it, and, when dropped to the deck, the circle folded into a crescent shape. From the vantage point of circling terns it looked like the world's largest sea gull, and the entire colony went berserk.

What makes the success of the tern repopulation even more exquisite for Steve Kress is the fact of their extraordinary annual migration. During August arctic terns, young and adult alike, leave Machias Seal Island and embark on a flight that continues to flabbergast man. Joining together with members of their species who have nested elsewhere along the North American coast, they cross the Atlantic, fly down the west coast of Europe and Africa, spend their winter between South Africa and the Antarctic Circle, only to return the following spring. Their migration covers a staggering twenty-two thousand miles.

It was a treat to have met people so much in the forefront of creative ecology—particularly a married couple as witty and energetic and articulate as Steve Kress and Evie Weinstein. At the end of our blustery conversation on Machias Seal Island, I asked Kress to summarize for me the larger goal of his work, the idea of which, incidentally, he has exported to the Galápagos, Hawaii, New Zealand, Ireland, California, and Japan.

"Humans are part of the system," began Kress. "We have affected it by our presence, but we should *continue* to affect it because our effect doesn't always have to be a negative one.

A pair of razorbilled auks.

"Generally, the result of human occupation of the land is an impoverishment of the wildlife species. The rare species end up being displaced or locally extirpated or even extinguished as in the cases of the great auk, Labrador duck, Carolina paroquet, and ivory-billed woodpecker. My belief is that our presence does not have to always lead to impoverishment. Our goal is to design management strategies that actually increase the diversity of species. That's what we really are all about."

Soon it was our turn to walk out to the blinds on the western shore of the island. Once inside the makeshift plywood shack, we slid open its windows. What a sight! A photographer's dream. As Dicken put it, "What a photo op!"

Not twenty feet away were scores of puffins and razorbills, both members of the auk family. Although the razorbills have their own charm with their lush black and white plumage and a finely drawn white ring around their bills, it is to the puffin one's lens is drawn. Like an avian Emmett Kelly, they are at once so comical and so sad looking. They waddle about as if they were wearing galoshes. Their mouths are filled with half a dozen neatly folded herring, which is all the more amazing when you realize that they have to catch them one at a time. When they fly, their short, stubby wings beat as often as four hundred times a minute, and they hurtle along like flying footballs.

Dicken, the logger, later added his version of the scene to the log: "The puffins make a moaning sound like a cow lowing or a small homeowner chain saw running with a plugged air filter and a dull chain."

Seven

MISS FOURTH OF JULY

Betsy sat on the brightwork box, which serves as the perch for *Consolation*'s helmsman. Eliza stood between her and the wheel. Learning to steer by compass goes against a novice's instinct because the steering wheel and the compass card turn confusingly in the opposite directions. But Eliza was determined and Betsy is a good teacher. Eliza is an only child and as a result, I think, tends to have a near-adult ability to concentrate. During her first lesson, she was watching the elusive compass card with such a dogged resolve that if a buoy had been in harm's way she would have run right smack into it.

Aiming for the Cross Island Narrows, Machias Bay, Eliza gets a lesson in seamanship.

She was wearing a blue anorak, hood up against the chill of the afternoon, and was steering roughly in the direction of the Cross Island Narrows at the eastern entrance to Machias Bay. We were somewhere between Machias Seal Island and Machiasport on the mainland. The sea was boisterous without being rough. We were making a respectable six knots under gray skies. Off to starboard we saw a platoon of five colorful sea kayaks. They seemed rather far off shore for their size, but I guess that is part of the fun of this newly rediscovered sport. Their progress flushed a baddling of at least a hundred eider ducks. The short, stocky ducks frantically struggled to be airborne. The black and white bodies of the eiders made a sharp contrast to the Day-Glo outfitted kayakers. Alternately flapping and sailing, they flew low over the water until we could no longer see them.

Wisps of Eliza's white blonde hair escaped her hood and framed her face. I felt a surge of pride as I saw the intensity she brought to learning something new. For me, part of doing this trip was to introduce Eliza to the cruising world Betsy and I so enjoy. She had, of course, sailed with us before. Her first overnight, I remember, involved a rough crossing of the Gulf Stream between Fort Lauderdale and the Bahamas. It was a sick-making passage. There were two other children aboard who felt perfectly awful. Their parents did, too. While all four of them were in—to use a polite word—discomfort, and the rest of us were pointedly staying above decks in the fresh air, seven-year-old Eliza sat alone at the saloon table wolfing down Lipton's Oodles of Noodles and chattering away about when we could anchor and go snorkeling.

"A little to the right. There you go. Good. Hold her steady right there." I looked up from my Dick Francis novel. Eliza's head was still bowed, her eyes glued to the compass. Betsy continued her patient instruction, "That's right. Try to keep as close to 330 degrees as you can."

Suddenly I heard a loud "Oh, shit!" from the other direction. I jumped out of my seat in time to see Dicken, up forward, dive toward the lee rail. He nearly went overboard in the bargain. There was a small, significant splash. "Damn, damn, damn," Dicken repeated as he plunked down on the cabin trunk, his head in his hands. "T-h-a-t," he said slowly, gesturing vaguely toward the navy blue water of the Atlantic, "*was* the only winch handle that raises the main."

One didn't need to be Sir Francis Chichester to appreciate the import of what Dicken was saying. With the winch handle permanently stored in Davy Jones's locker, we could always lower the mainsail, but we could not operate the mast-mounted winch to get the heavy sail back up.

Now, our first priority was to find a new winch handle. We were not exactly in the region of snazzy ship chandleries, yacht clubs, and marinas catering to sailboats. We would be lucky enough to find a nearby boatyard; it would be a miracle if we found a place selling a handle for an expensive Barient winch. After consultation with Hank and Jan Taft's *A Cruising Guide to the Maine Coast,* a book which I have come to think of as the sine qua non of our ship's library, I could see that our closest bet was the historic little town of Machias, population roughly twenty-five hundred. We knew we would not find a sign there saying Visiting Yachtsmen: Sale on Winch Handles—50% Off. We did, however, hope to locate a good hardware store where we might find the component parts to jury-rig one.

The decision was made. In no time we passed Bucks Harbor where Jasper Cates had had his "flap" with the prospective oil refinery, and by 2:00 P.M., we were peacefully anchored in the middle of the Machias River off Machiasport.

It was only four miles up to Machias. Dicken, Eliza, and I left Betsy water coloring and looking after the boat. We stood on the dusty shoulder of Route 92, and Eliza stuck out her thumb. When it came to hitchhiking, we had become experts. Our ace-in-the-hole naturally was Eliza—a fact, which she quickly glommed onto, and about which she had become mildly resentful (but so far not mutinous). Secretly I thought she enjoyed her status—it's nice to be able to do something better than your parents can.

In any case Dicken and I trolled her front and center and tried ourselves to be as inconspicuous as possible. After just a few days of not shaving, Dicken and I start to look like terrorists. Neither one of us would have had a snowball's chance in hell of being picked up, but with Eliza as bait our luck had been phenomenal.

In other situations, too, I had thought of Eliza as a sort of roving ambassador, a minister without portfolio. If there was a laconic, stern-faced stranger I wanted to ask questions of, I would surreptitiously dispatch Eliza first. And, like the good envoy she was, she could disarm even the crustiest of coots.

A brown Plymouth, the first car to come by, skidded to a halt; Eliza could chalk up another success.

"Where ya headed?" called an elderly man out his wife's open window.

"Machias," Eliza replied, and we piled in.

Paul as it turned out was a lobsterman, semi-retired, and Marie was his wife. You can run into some serious friendliness down east, and after some thought Paul recommended the True Value hardware store as our best bet, and Marie recommended Helen's Restaurant, which she assured us served "the best strawberry pie in Washington County if not the whole state." When we reached the True Value, Marie said they would be happy to wait for us and give us a ride back to *Consolation.* I thanked her, but I said it might take us a long time to sort out the missing winch handle problem. With more thank yous, we said good-bye.

The fact that the True Value hardware store in Machias did not sell winch handles for cruising yachts came as no surprise. What was surprising was how difficult it was to concoct a workable substitute. With the enthusiastic assistance of two salesmen and three other customers, we eventually put together a contrivance that I am confident would have made Rube Goldberg green. We combined a square drain plug, a reducing bushing, two nuts, and a pipe wrench, and voilà! we had ourselves a winch handle.

Rather pleased with ourselves, we paid for our purchases moments before closing time and stepped out into the late afternoon sunshine. Eliza agreed once again to front for us. No sooner had she arranged her face into a suitably entreating expression than our old friends Marie and Paul pulled up in their Plymouth. Were these people so incredibly nice that they secretly waited for us anyway? I began to suspect so.

We piled back into the big sedan and headed for our next stop, the A & P. Along the way Paul pointed out Burnham Tavern, which had a sign outside that advertised:

Drink for the Thirsty
Food for the Hungry
Lodging for the Weary
and
Good Keeping for Horses

"Eliza," said Paul, "You're looking at the oldest building east of the Penobscot River. It was built way back in 1770 before the American Revolution. I wonder if you folks would be interested in the story of how Machias became the birthplace of the American navy?"

"Oh, come on, Paul," Marie said, "they've got better things to do than listen to that old story . . ."

No, we insisted (not 100 percent sincerely), we *did* want to hear "that old story." But we were wrong to be skeptical, and Marie was wrong to poach. Paul gave us a wonderfully rich account of a piece of Maine history. It went something like this:

"Remember Ralph Waldo Emerson's Concord Hymn?" Paul asked. He quoted a stanza from memory:

By the rude bridge that arched the flood,
Their flag to April's breeze unfurled,
Here once the embattled farmers stood,
And fired the shot heard round the world.

"Emerson" Paul told us, "was writing about the Battle of Lexington and Concord, of course, but less than two months after that important battle something happened right here in Machias that was pretty darned important, too. The British sent an order to Machias for some lumber they needed to build a new barracks in Boston. This was just a routine request, but since the people of Machias had already heard about what the patriots in Concord and Lexington had done, they decided to consider this request more carefully than usual.

"An informal town meeting was held along the banks of the brook, which runs through town. Like most such meetings it ended up getting a little heated because everyone had an opinion and nobody was afraid to voice his. Finally, one Benjamin Foster got so sick of all the backing and forthing that he leapt across the brook and shouted, 'Those of you who want to kiss the boots of the bloody Redcoats stay where you are. Those of you who want to enlist in the cause of the Patriots, I challenge you, come and join me.' In the end all the men of Machias were on Foster's side of the brook, and it is known to this day as Foster's Rubicon.

"A few days later a British cutter, the *Margaretta,* armed with four four-pounders and sixteen guns, arrived in Machias escorting two freight-laden sloops, the *Polly* and the *Unity.* A group of forty Machias colonists shanghaied the *Unity,* chased the *Margaretta* until they caught up with her in Machias Bay, and overwhelmed her crew. The patriots were only armed with pitchforks, which were readily handy because it was haying season. Everyone was surprised that only five men lost their lives in the battle. One of them, the captain of the *Margaretta,* died that night in Burnham Tavern, which you just passed.

The defunct Machiasport Packing and Canning Company. Historic Machiasport has seen the birth of the American navy and the death of the sardine industry.

"The victors transferred *Margaretta*'s weapons to the *Unity,* and right away they rechristened her the *Machias Liberty.*

". . . Which is how this town earned the right to call itself the Birthplace of the United States Navy."

The jury-rigged winch handle worked, but just barely. We managed to haul the 345-square-foot mainsail all the way up the mast. But the effort was inconvenient enough to continue the search for a store-bought model. With that in mind we set sail for Pettegrow's Boatyard in Starboard at the end of the peninsula that separates Englishman and Machias Bays.

On arrival Dicken and I rowed ashore in search of Mr. Pettegrow. Betsy and Eliza stayed aboard to experiment with shipboard bread baking. The field behind Pettegrow's boat shed was sprinkled with buttercups and bordered by thickets of rosa rugosa, and we were encouraged to see a number of small sailboats on cradles. Perhaps Mr. Pettegrow could lay his hands on a winch handle.

The *Monica and Melanie,* a weary-looking quahog dragger, was on the ways, out of the water. (According to Dicken, who is my most reliable source on all such matters, a quahog, pronounced *ko'hog,* is the Indian word for hard-shelled clams. Littlenecks, cherrystones, and chowders are the *commercial* names for quahogs and are based on size alone—littlenecks being the smallest. Otherwise, they are just bivalves by any other name.) Pettegrow was nowhere to be seen, but a Bert Preston popped his head over the *Monica and Melanie*'s gunwale and greeted us.

"Richard'll be back in a minute."

Made in the shade on a hot summer's day. Pettegrow's Boatyard, Starboard Cove.

"Thanks," I answered. "What's wrong with your boat?"

"Oh, tain't mine," Preston laughed. "Glad about it, too. Engine on this boat's been breaking down so often. Why we've had to be towed in twice in the last week. It's starting to get embarrassing!"

Like two old buddies huddled around the pot-bellied stove at the general store, Dicken and Bert jawed agreeably about weighty matters: diesel engines, quahogs, and the difficulty of figuring offshore currents. I sat on the bottom rung of a wooden ladder in the shade of the *Monica and Melanie* and listened.

Bert Preston is a man who looks like he has endured more than one nor'-wester, as his deeply lined face attests. Wearing a bushy blond handle-bar mustache and an oil-stained University of Maine baseball cap, Preston had the air of the sea dog who had seen it all.

"Heard a good one the other day from this guy Joe Perham, who makes a living telling Maine stories. Can you beat that? Getting paid to tell jokes?

"Anyway, there was this old farmer who lived over near Gilead on the Maine–New Hampshire border. That road there, the Evans Notch Road (which is closed in the winter, by the way), wanders back and forth across the state line so many times you hardly know where you are.

"Not too long ago they re-surveyed, and they discovered that this farmer had always lived on the New Hampshire side of the border. Well, by golly, he was eighty-eight years old, and he always thought that he'd been living in Maine. When they told him, he said, 'Thank the Lord! I don't think I could've stood another one of those Maine winters.' "

Bert Preston of the *Monica and Melanie*.

Richard Pettegrow interrupted our laughter with the news that, no, he did not have a winch handle. We followed him into his boathouse where he offered us each a soda from an antique Coke machine. He scribbled a name on a slip of paper. "A friend of mine in Jonesport has a boatyard; maybe he'll have what you're looking for."

We spent the night in Bunker Hole after a noon-time stop at the fabled crescent beach on Roque Island before hastening to Jonesport for the Fourth of July festivities and that elusive winch handle. Roque, I should interject, is a mandatory stop for cruising yachtsmen venturing east of Schoodic Point. Owned by the fifty-eight adult members of the Gardner and Monks families (the Gardners are the same as those who endowed the Gardner Museum in Boston), Roque has four houses, two three-hundred-pound pigs, fifteen sheep, assorted cows, turkeys, pigeons, chickens, and three horses. The owners take great pride in the near self-sufficiency of Roque, and they generously permit what I call "honor-system trespassing" on their magnificent mile-long white sand beach.

Above all, we were not about to miss Jonesport's annual super-dee-duper World's Fastest Lobster Boat Race and Fourth of July parade. All along the coast, we had been admonished: "Whatever you do, don't miss the lobster boat race in Jonesport!" We dropped anchor in Moosabec Reach east of the bridge that links Jonesport and Beals Island. It is no accident that the races are held here; more lobster boats are built in the Jonesport–Beals Island area than anywhere else in Maine.

The fabled mile-long, white sand beach at Roque Island: A mandatory stop for cruising yachtsmen venturing east of Schoodic Point.

When we were satisfied that we would have an unrestricted view of the racecourse, we rowed ashore in *Hoggie* for the parade. We climbed onto the dock and there, nailed to a piling, was the line-up for the sixteen different events. The classes included everything from "Lobster Outboards—50–100HP" to a whole

Consolation **at anchor in Mud Hole, Great Wass Island between Western and Eastern bays.**

range of events restricted by boat length ("28–32′ Diesel, 33–36′ Diesel, 37–40′ Diesel") to "Free For All Diesel" and finally "WFLB"—The World's Fastest Lobster Boat Race. I could not help but notice that there were a lot of men called Beal competing in the various events. Among the fifty-nine entrants were Loren F. Beal, Calvin Beal, Jr., Ike Beal, Osmond Beal, Glenn Beal, Robert Beal, Mike Beal, Merle Beal, Robert Beal, and the man we'd been told was the odds-on favorite, Benny Beal.

As I read the line-up, a deep-voiced lobster boat rumbled up to the dock. She was the most pristine working boat I had ever seen—so immaculate, in fact, that I wondered how often she actually hauled pots. When I spotted the name emblazoned on her bow, I knew why. I was getting a close-up view of *Benny's Bitch*, four-time winner of The World's Fastest Lobster Boat Race. I had heard grumblings about *Benny's Bitch*—that she was strictly a racing boat and consequently unfair competition. Grousing notwithstanding, Benny raced her every year, and kept winning.

While picturesque, Jonesport's Sawyer Memorial Congregational Church is probably less of a magnet for visitors than the World's Fastest Lobster Boat Race.

I could see Benny himself on board with a man I learned was his son-in-law. Benny seemed a little preoccupied when I approached him, so I introduced myself to the son-in-law, and we chatted about the race. He predicted that Benny would win again, and told me (somewhat unnecessarily, I thought) that his father-in-law "takes real good care of his boat." When I mentioned the gigantic Beal family, he grinned mightily. "Yeah," he said, chuckling, "you're right about there being a slew of Beals. Sometimes I think this place is so in-bred that in another decade we're gonna be back to Neanderthal man."

Benny's son-in-law suggested we visit a Jonesport resident named Andy Swift, who is a nationally known practitioner of an esoteric business—that of restoring antique fire trucks. He calls his company Firefly. Before the parade Betsy, Eliza, and I trooped up the road east of town to pay an unannounced visit on Swift.

His wife Kathy greeted us at the door. She was terribly welcoming. She told us that Andy had "walking pneumonia" and that he was upstairs resting. Over our strenuous objections she said, "No, no. I'll wake him up."

He came downstairs, tousled but also welcoming, and took us out to his workshop where he was currently restoring a 1916 American La France. The care and attention he put into his work was immediately apparent. The restoration process, he told us, can sometimes take as long as three years. I wanted to ask him how much he charged, but, uncharacteristically, I refrained.

At work on a 1916 American La France, Andy Swift lovingly restores antique fire trucks.

"My thing is to make them look exactly as they did originally. I pride myself on the accuracy of my restorations," Swift said. Apparently others do too, because museums and fire companies all over the country ship fire vehicles for him to work on. He primarily restores horse-drawn and hand pumpers with their often elaborate decorative paintings. "They were made to look so beautiful and ornate," he explained, "because they were the pride of not only their fire companies but the whole town."

"Besides," he added, "fire engines are fun because—like apple pie and George Washington—all Americans love them."

We met Dicken in time for the parade, and he had a surprise for us. Somewhere in Jonesport he had found a friendly (and open) machine shop. There he had taken one of *Consolation*'s spare winch handles and ground it down to fit the square shape of the mast's winch. "We're back in business!" he said with justifiable pride in his ingenuity.

The Fourth of July Parade, Jonesport: An ungrapeful marcher thinks unkind thoughts about his mother.

The Jonesport Fourth of July parade was a jingoist's dream. Under a brilliant blue sky, the first of the parade's many color guards marched behind the Jonesport police car. Following it were a string of convertibles bearing more beauty queens than an Atlantic City runway. Miss Fourth of July sat on the trunk lid of the first car. Then came her "court": the First Princess, Second Princess, and Third Princess. There was a Jr. Miss Fourth of July and her court, a Miss Beals Island and her court and . . . well, you get the idea.

I met an English bulldog at the parade called Maybeline. She was wearing a pair of American flag panties and sported two additional flags taped to her collar. Maybeline attracted plenty of attention and, when passersby stopped to pat her, she closed her eyes in the dreamy way cats do when they are scratched behind their ears.

We saw a platoon of miniature motorized lobster boats pass, driven by Shriners wearing purple fezzes and wielding scimitars; an antique fire truck driven by our new friend Andy Swift; marching bands galore; an enormous navy blue tractor-trailer owned by Maine Wild Blueberries; and—for reasons known only to his mother—a small boy covered from head to toe with purple balloons, who was supposed to look like a bunch of grapes and who instead looked very unhappy. A man walking behind him, who may or may not have been his father, wore a baseball cap with the following printed on the front: My wife ran away with my best friend and I miss him.

After the parade The World's Fastest Lobster Boat Race was somewhat anticlimactic. It came as no surprise that most of the races were won by Beals, and *Benny's Bitch* won the grand prize one more time. The only drama was that Eliza spent the whole race with her head in a bucket. Since *Consolation* was peacefully anchored, Betsy's diagnosis was a stomach bug. And, indeed, it quickly passed.

Eight

DUNGEON THICK O' FOG

It was not the densest fog in the history of seacoast Maine nor by any means the longest lasting (remember Neil Corbett having to fuel the Little River fog horn for 525 continuous hours), but it was our first encounter with a legendary Maine pea-souper. A monochromatic pall lay athwart us like a saturated shroud. There was no horizon, no sea or sky, just a gray rain cloud within which we navigated with a mixture of trust and trepidation. Everything was wet; droplets of condensing water vapor clung to our sweaters, hair, the sails, and dripped from the rigging. Dicken's week-old beard was speckled with water droplets, which made him look like some demented sea dog.

We were heading for Corea on the far side of Gouldsboro Bay when the fog rolled in. We read in the Tafts' cruising guide that Corea Harbor was hard to enter in the best of conditions. Their description was sprinkled with admonitions like: ". . . unmarked rocks and ledges . . . not an easy harbor to enter . . . nasty rock . . . avoid coming in at dead high, dead low, or in poor visibility." Without fog it sounded dicey enough; with the fog, it was enough to daunt Leif Ericson. And it was high tide.

The all-encompassing pea-souper made for a good test of our dead reckoning skills. Gingerly we navigated from buoy to buoy. We paid close attention to our compass course and our distance-made-good. We tried to compensate for the effects of the flooding tide and its associated current. Above all we listened for the toll of the bell buoys, the irregular dissonance of the four-noted gong buoys, and the eerie cry of the whistle buoys. One of those sounds would beckon us to our next way point.

Duncan and Ware warned of the pitfalls of navigating to the Siren of an elusive buoy: "Fog seems to do strange things to sound. Never count on picking up a whistle or bell when it is to leeward of you. Also, 'dead spots' seem to form, and the vigorous bellow of a horn ten miles away may be inaudible within three miles of the station yet may nearly blow you off the deck within two miles."

The irony of navigating from buoy to buoy is that, if you are very good at it, you run the risk of colliding with the very buoy you are trying to find. We did not do that, but we came very close twice.

The fog was a mite thick: Corea on the Schoodic Peninsula. Can you find *Consolation* and *Hoggie* in the mull?

We heard Whistler *CE* to starboard and eventually spotted the red and white buoy when we were nearly on top of it. I kept the forward watch, taking care to keep one arm around the forestay as a hedge against the unexpected bump. Dicken steered, and Betsy tracked our progress on the most detailed chart we had, No. 13324. When I looked aft, I could not see either of them through the impenetrable cloud.

As a boy Dicken had learned the sailor's trick of heading for a bold shore in the fog. The theory is that you will hear what Maine fishermen call the "rote," that is the waves crashing against the rocks, and see the faint white line of the surf in sufficient time to tack, thus avoiding the collision of boat and rock, which the rock invariably wins.

We made, therefore, for the bold shore of Western Island. When we saw it, we changed course and followed the shoreline just beyond the crashing breakers. Rocks and ledges guard the western approach to Corea so we made for Youngs Point and hugged that shore until we finally entered the harbor. Corea Harbor is snug, tiny, and has little room for other than its resident fleet of about forty-five lobster boats and draggers.

We carefully poked around the crowded anchorage looking for a spot. A boy about twelve years old in a skiff emerged out of the gloom and kindly directed us to an unused mooring next to a lobster boat called *Sea Smoke.* Her name seemed all the more appropriate considering what we had just sailed through. Dicken deftly maneuvered *Consolation* to the seaweed-y buoy, and I snagged the pennant with a boat hook. I confess I breathed a sigh of relief when I made the bitter end fast.

I lifted the heavy lid of the icebox and, supporting it with the top of my head, chipped a few shards from a new block of Jonesport ice. "Chip off a new block," I thought, as I poured generous drinks for the grown-ups—rum for Dicken, bourbon for Betsy, and scotch for me—and a Schweppes raspberry ginger ale for Eliza. We settled down for a cozy, fog-enshrouded (and we felt well-deserved) cocktail hour.

Dicken volunteered for galley duty and began preparations for pork chops and twice-baked potatoes.

Between Betsy and Dicken, *Consolation* could not have had two more inventive or original chefs. Cooking is not my strong suit, I should interject, although I would urge anyone to sample my personal *spécialité,* an often underrated Fettucine Alfredo prepared with American cheese.

Dicken, who is known as "Chef Eddie" when he dons his cooking apron, specializes in the creative recycling of leftovers. He prides himself on being able to use everything again, often making the second go-round more delicious than the first. Chef Eddie's culinary credo is simple: onions, cheese, and especially A.1. steak sauce should be part of every meal. As Yogi Berra would say, Dicken's dinner was déjà vu all over again. The twice-baked potatoes were stuffed with onions, cheese, and topped with A.1., and they were delicious.

In the dim light of an early Monday morning I looked out the porthole above my bunk and saw nothing. The fog had lingered; we were completely socked in. Even our neighbor *Sea Smoke* had disappeared. We had heard the Corea lobster fleet leave at dawn, but we had heard most of them return within the hour. If it was too foggy for a Corea lobsterman, it was *really* foggy.

Corea.

After breakfast Eliza, Dicken, and I rowed ashore and almost immediately ran into Joe Young, Jr., a lanky, local fisherman.

"Did you come in last night?" Joe asked.

"We sure did," said Eliza, "and, boy, was it foggy!"

"Ever sailed in here before?"

"No," I answered, "first time."

"Oh . . ." I began to sense a hint of regard in Joe's voice.

"It sounded like everyone came back in this morning," I said. "It must have been pretty bad out there."

Joe's eyes widened, but he did not answer me directly. "Didn't you hear about the *Lou Ann*?"

I told him we had not.

"She was coming back in the fog this morning, filled with fish. Headed for the Stinson Cannery in Prospect Harbor. She was an old sardine carrier, the *Lou Ann,* a 70-footer. They said the captain took a nap and told the mate to wake him when they neared Schoodic Point."

Joe paused before continuing. "Well, he didn't. She went right up on Old Man ledge not more than two miles from where we're standing now. The *Lou Ann* sank this morning. Sank like a stone. The boys barely had time to save themselves." Whoa, I thought, there but for the grace of God. . . .

Then he said what we had both been thinking. "I guess you people were pretty lucky." It was a sobering moment.

Joe offered to show us around in his brown Buick: Prospect Harbor (home of the Stinson Seafood Company), Gouldsboro (through which Route 1, Maine's principal tourist artery, crawls), the tony Grindstone Neck area of Winter Harbor, and the rocky tip of the peninsula itself, Schoodic Point. Having no idea how much we would be able to see in the fog, I gratefully accepted Joe's offer anyway. Eliza, Dicken, and I climbed in, and we set off with headlights emphatically on.

We had frequently heard the expressions "thick o' fog" and the more ominous sounding "dungeon thick o' fog," but I was in a fog myself about which term to use when. I turned to Joe for a lesson in correct usage. He had already told me that his grandfather was a rum-runner and used to take him into the woods to cut spruce boughs and steam them to form the lathe for half-moon lobster traps. He seemed salty enough to answer the vexing question when is it foggy enough to be considered dungeon thick o' fog?

I got an answer and then some. I was given a full treatise on fog. Fog mull apparently is the term used by the cognoscenti to refer to the general condition of fog, no matter how thick. The varying degrees of severity of a fog mull are in ascending order: *kinda soupy, a mite thick, thick o' fog,* and finally the dreaded *dungeon thick o' fog.* "When a Maine lobsterman says dungeon thick o' fog," he said, "check to make sure you can still see the end of your nose."

Joe told us about *smoky sou'westers* and *sea smoke,* how the fog *scales up* when it *burns off,* and the fact that fog is nothing more than a big, wet cloud that rests on the earth—both land and water. He said that although Corea has its share of fog, the record is held by Petit Manan Island. 'Titm'nan, as Petit Manan is universally called, is an offshore island east of Corea.

" 'Titm'nan has an *average* of 250 hours of fog each July and August," Joe declared in what sounded to my ears like a boast. (I have noticed that Mainers have a peculiar habit of bragging about what visitors might consider local liabilities. Mainers take great pride, for instance, in the harshness of their winters, the fogginess of their summers, and how cold their water is, no matter the season.

We were driving down the road that leads to the tip of the Schoodic Peninsula. Had it not been for the fog, we would have been able to see Bar Harbor and Mount Desert Island across Frenchman Bay to the west. As I looked out the window, I could barely see the coastline the road to Schoodic hugged. The fog put me into a kind of reverie, and I was reminded of an apocryphal Maine sea story. It goes like this: "Only reason I found my way back into the harbor was that I'd had the foresight to stick my knife in the fog, on my way out, to mark the entrance."

It was through Joe Young, Jr., that I met Joe Young, Sr., and through them both that I met Marcia Spurling.

How to describe Marcia Spurling? Cantankerous? Crotchety? Yes, both are accurate, but there was something more—a secret smile perhaps behind her peppery pronouncements. Marcia is eighty-seven years old and a spinster. (Yes, I know that it is politically incorrect to use terms like spinster and old maid just because someone chose never to marry, but Marcia Spurling really *is* a spinster.)

Marcia Spurling: "I suppose," she said, "you want to pester me with questions about my life . . ."

She received us in the house in which she has lived for the last eighty years, quickly pointing out that she spent her first seven years in the house next door. She sat in a rocking chair, her knitting in her lap, her white hair pulled back in a bun.

"You can sit wherever you want," she said by way of greeting Eliza, Joe Young, Sr., and me. "I'm too old to get up for you youngsters," she said with a glance at Joe, who, I happened to know, was a grandfather.

I thanked her for letting us visit.

"Speak up! Speak up!" she replied crossly, but she winked in Eliza's direction as if to let her know that she wasn't really the ogre she pretended to be.

I showed her my tape recorder, and, nodding in acquiescence, she said, "I suppose you want to pester me with questions about my life, huh? I thought so. Well, I was born right here in Corea during an earthquake. The next day it snowed. And that pretty well sums up my life."

MARIA S.
DIANE SUE

The fog lifts.

I thought for a minute that she was actually going to stop right there, but after a pause she continued.

"Five years ago I broke my hip and had to spend two weeks in the hospital in Ellsworth. That was the only time I spent a night outside Corea in my whole life." I was dumbfounded. Was it really possible to meet someone in the 1990s who had spent her entire life in a village of less than 375 people? Three hundred and seventy-five people is, after all, what a smallish city apartment building holds. My astonishment was so transparent that Marcia was unable to stifle a grin.

When I asked how Corea had changed in her lifetime, she responded firmly, "I don't like any of the changes since they brought in electric lights. Lights or no lights, though, life is hard here. I never had a car. If you wanted groceries during the winter, why you just had to walk for them even if it was snowing."

"Yes, Marcia," Joe Young put in, "but you had your sled."

"That's true, Joe," she said sweetly while aiming dagger eyes at him.

"I didn't have many jobs in my life," she continued. "Once, though, I worked for some rusticators. I tidied and cleaned for them—they were summer people and could afford it. The lady of the house wasn't very nice, but I'd just feed her drinks, one after another. Long as I did that, she stayed pretty good-natured."

"Don't fall overboard," was her advice for Eliza. "The mackerel'll get you!"

And, finally, this from a woman who had spent eighty-seven years within a stone's throw of the sea: "I always hated boats. My father sailed a coasting schooner before he became a lobsterman, but I always hated boats. I wouldn't have crossed Corea Harbor in your boat. I couldn't swim. I could've walked on the water better'n I could've swam."

Marcia had started speaking in the past tense. It occurred to me that I was hearing someone composing her own epitaph.

As I followed Joe Young out the door, he said, "Did you ever hear of the writer Louise Dickinson Rich?" I certainly had. Rich wrote a series of charming books about Maine including *We Took to the Woods, The Coast of Maine, State O' Maine,* and *The Peninsula.*

"She and Marcia were friends," Joe said. "In fact, she stayed with Marcia the winter she wrote *The Peninsula.*"

The mention of Rich's name triggered the memory of a quotation from one of her books. Rich had written: "Nowhere that I know do the past and the present get along as amicably as they do on the coast of Maine." She wrote it, of course, in a different context, but I wondered as I headed back to *Consolation* how Rich's assessment applied to the extraordinary life of Marcia Spurling.

Rowing back to the boat, we passed a disgruntled-looking man with sunglasses on despite the fog. It was low tide, and Tom Bridges crouched on a slippery wrack-covered rock using a hoe for balance. Behind him was his boat, a gill-netter named *Old Yellow Bird.* She looked like it had been a few years since she had been a young yellow bird. Her paint was peeling, her waterline, algae-infested, and the only trace of her name were the remaining five letters stuck to her stern: **YEL BI**

Tom Bridges did not look much happier than his boat. He explained that he had just been fined $5,000 by the Canadians for being three-quarters of a mile inside Canadian Territorial Waters carrying a catch of four thousand pounds of fish the Canadians claimed were theirs. They towed him for nine hours to Grand Manan Island, a Canadian island off West Quoddy Head. After which, they kept him under armed guard for another twenty-four hours before he could be brought before a judge.

When he appeared before the magistrate, Bridges pleaded not guilty, but the judge found otherwise. Bridges reported with disgust that in pronouncing the sentence the judge had decreed: "You owe $5,000 to the Prime Minister, and the Queen gets the fish."

Nine

"GEESH, DAD, WHO BUILT THIS PLACE?"

"IF YOU DON'T LIKE THE WEATHER in New England," Samuel Clemens once said, "wait ten minutes." That may be a bit of an exaggeration where a mull is concerned, but, after two thick o' fog days, all of a sudden it was one of those perfectly spectacular days which made one think "Fog? What's fog?" The sea was the darkest possible shade of blue and so was the sky. Altocumulus clouds sailed high above, whitecaps dotted the water, and *Consolation,* her mainsail double reefed, screamed up Frenchman Bay. We were beating into exhilarating thirty-five-knot winds, bound for Sorrento at the head of the bay.

To the east, breakers crashed against Schoodic Point. The swells came from

An "old sea" crashes against Big Moose Island at the tip of Schoodic Point. To the west, Mount Desert Island.

***Consolation*, her mainsail double reefed, screamed up Frenchman Bay.**

way beyond the limits of the Gulf of Maine far out in the Atlantic. Mainers speak of this as an "old sea." Its surf battered the low, flat outcropping of granite just as it had for the intervening tens of thousands of years since the ice had melted. To the west rose the mounded humps of Mount Desert Island, dominated by Cadillac Mountain towering above the unruly seas. Ahead of us lay Bar Harbor. Across the whitecaps I could see the *Bluenose* gathering way, beginning her daily voyage to Yarmouth, Nova Scotia. While the ferry may be unpopular with lobstermen—she tends to be oblivious to the amount of lobster gear her propellers destroy—a trip on the *Bluenose* saves a Canadian-bound traveler 750 miles of driving.

We were running fast, our gunwales—and in occasional gusts the cockpit itself—were in the water. It was what James Joyce once described as a "scrotum-tightening sea." The angle of *Consolation*'s heel was almost 40 degrees. Spray flew over the windward bow and drenched us in spite of the canvas dodger. Someone once said that the perfect crewman should be as strong as a gorilla, as agile as a cat, and every tooth should be a marlinespike. Maybe we did not satisfy that profile exactly, but there was plenty of Yo-ho-ho on deck!

Although we could have eased a sheet or two and fallen off the wind a hair, we were pushing *Consolation* to perform. And performing she was! She is a powerful,

Blessed with a cast-iron stomach, Eliza chooses, in heavy weather, to remain below. She busies herself reading and will occasionally dip a carrot stick into a jar of Russian dressing.

fast sloop, and sailing her as hard as we were was a breathtaking experience.

We were in the lee of Waukeag Neck about a mile from the village of Sorrento before Mark Twain's weather could change again.

I continue to be amazed and entertained by both the variety and singularity of place names in Maine. A few days before we had lunched near a promontory with the unusual name Tumbledown Dick Head, and on this day we had passed an island called Junk of Pork.

While there is only one Junk of Pork Island (that I know of) in the Maine archipelago, there are an astonishing number of islands with the same names. There are, for instance, twenty-six Bear Islands, as well as fourteen Hog Islands, twelve Seal Coves, eight Crow Islands, and a Crow Cove. There are three Mooses, two Minks, and two Mouse Islands. There's a Flea Island and two Fox Islands; a Dog, a Deer, and a Duck; thirteen Sheep and twenty-two Ram Islands. There's Upper Goose, Lower Goose, and The Goslings. Ten Pound Island and Pound of Tea. Three Smuttynose Islands and an Irony.

Arrayed in what almost seems like a defensive semicircle around Bar Harbor are Sheep Porcupine Island, Burnt Porcupine Island, Long Porcupine Island, and Bald Porcupine Island. Could this, I asked myself, be some peculiar porcupine patrol protecting Bar Harbor from pugnacious porgies?

About as often as I asked myself that, I wondered if that longtime Maine rusticator during one of his outings on his motorboat, *Fidelity*, had ever negotiated the narrow passage between George Island and Bush Island?

We had a trek ahead of us to get to Sorrento's market. It was a one-half mile walk through a sweet-smelling balsam woods to Route 185 where we would be able to hitchhike the rest of the way into the village.

Consistent with long-established practice, we trolled Eliza for a ride. A car whizzed past, then another and another. The drivers kept their eyes face-front, avoiding ours. What could be wrong, I wondered? Dicken and I had not shaved for a few days, but that was nothing new. Eliza looked especially pretty, I thought, although her hair—like ours—could have handled a wash. Eventually, as more cars passed, it dawned on me. The Saabs and Jeep Cherokees and Volvo station wagons whizzing by had license plates from Pennsylvania, Ohio, New York, Massachusetts—and not from Maine. With a sense of loss, I realized we were now in the land of the summer visitors, who had brought to Maine their baggage of urban fear instead of leaving it behind in Boston, New York, Cleveland, or Philadelphia.

I am being completely truthful when I report that the first Maine-tagged vehicle, a rusty pick-up driven by a young man with a spotted dog, hit the brakes when he saw us and called out the window, "Hop in the back, if you don't mind the mess!"

We had rounded Schoodic Point, and, just as we had been warned, the days of never seeing another sailboat, the nights of anchoring alone in a distant cove were over. Oh, we had much to look forward to: the majesty of nearby Mount Desert Island, for starters. And beyond: Penobscot, Muscongus, and Casco Bays; the outer islands—Matinicus, Monhegan, Damariscove, Seguin; towns and villages of interest and beauty like Castine and Camden and Kittery. There was

The Porcupine Islands guard Bar Harbor.

West Pond on the Schoodic Peninsula.

much to lure us on, but I knew I would miss down east Maine—and especially the down easters who had not treated us as strangers "from away" but who had welcomed us as friends.

We paid for our few purchases—milk, eggs, bread, orange juice—and arranged with the proprietor to keep them there while we looked around Sorrento.

Down the road apiece Eliza and I came upon a marvelous municipal edifice which housed the Sorrento Public Library. The architecture of the library had benefited, I guessed, from the generosity of a wealthy summer community around the turn of the century. It was a shingle-style affair with a grand round-arched portico. A porte cochère sheltered the entrance, above which was a Palladian window with a triptych of windows each divided into twenty-four lights, and capping it all was a delicately muntined fanlight.

In front of the library Eliza and I met an older woman walking her bicycle. Her groceries filled two red saddlebags mounted over the rear wheel. We never found out her name, but we would come to call her the Puzzle Woman.

Ralph Stanley in his small yard in Southwest Harbor: "I was one of the last people building wooden lobster boats," he said, "but I doubt I'll build another. Too expensive."

The bowsprit of a Friendship sloop built by Ralph Stanley in 1979 and his stunning restoration of a fifty-year-old Herreshoff.

A 30-foot pleasure launch based on a lobster boat hull under construction in the Stanley yard. Jim Livingston works on the cabin trunk ribs while Ralph's son, Richard, sands below the waterline.

The Puzzle Woman was a rusticator but a longtime one. She had raised seven children in Sorrento during the summers. Since they had all fledged, as she put it, she was cleaning out her house, sending childhood memories to the dump. She invited us for a visit anyway, saying, "Try to ignore the clutter."

On the way she told us something of Sorrento. Yes, the library had been built around the turn of the century—1892 to be exact. Waukeag Neck had been developed as a resort in the 1880s, something of a poor man's Bar Harbor but nevertheless grand in its own way, in part due to the enthusiasm of a promoter named Frank Jones. It was he who decided that "Sorrento" had more sex appeal than "Waukeag Neck" and changed the name. Grover Cleveland spent a summer in Sorrento when the resort hotels still thrived. More recently, Norman Mailer had.

When we reached her house, the Puzzle Woman showed Eliza a stack of jigsaw puzzles she had gathered to take to the dump and insisted that Eliza choose one as a gift. As tactfully as she could, Eliza tried to explain to her how inconvenient it would be to solve a jigsaw puzzle on a sailboat. But this dear mother of seven persisted. Eventually we left with a compromise gift better suited to shipboard life: a paperback copy of *Doctor Doolittle Tales.*

The next morning in the Northeast Harbor marina parking lot Dicken and I stumbled into a Hertz rent-a-car. It was very early; it would be an hour at least before the "rosy fingers" would rise above the mountains to the east and warm the protected harbor. We were making the obligatory pilgrimage, joining thousands of like-minded tourists, to watch the sunrise from the 1,532-foot peak of Cadillac Mountain in Acadia National Park on Mount Desert Island.

Dicken drove up the winding, crowded road. Behind us was a car from West Virginia, ahead, one from South Dakota; together we formed part of a long line snaking up to the summit of this national tourist destination. And I, bleary-eyed, made like the good tourist and read some of the history of Mount Desert courtesy of a National Park Service flyer.

We were ascending the highest mountain on the Atlantic coast between Canada and Brazil, I read. Cadillac Mountain was named for a man named Antoine Laumet, a personal favorite of Louis the XIV's. Laumet reinvented himself as Sieur Antoine de la Mothe Cadillac and with this elegant title (and a generous royal grant) moved his wife, family, and a retinue of servants and slaves to Mount Desert Island. He hoped to establish a feudal domain over the Indians. For unclear reasons his plan failed, so he moved to Detroit where he is best remembered as the namesake of an automobile. The year spent on Mount Desert, 1688, left a lasting impression, however: To his dying day he signed his name "Seigneur des Mont Deserts."

Eighty-four years earlier Samuel de Champlain had given Mount Desert its name. On September 5, 1604, Champlain—French explorer, geographer, and colonizer in the service of King Henry IV—ran his ship up on a shoal off Otter

The Precipice Trail on Champlain Mountain was temporarily closed so that a pair of peregrine falcons could raise their three chicks.

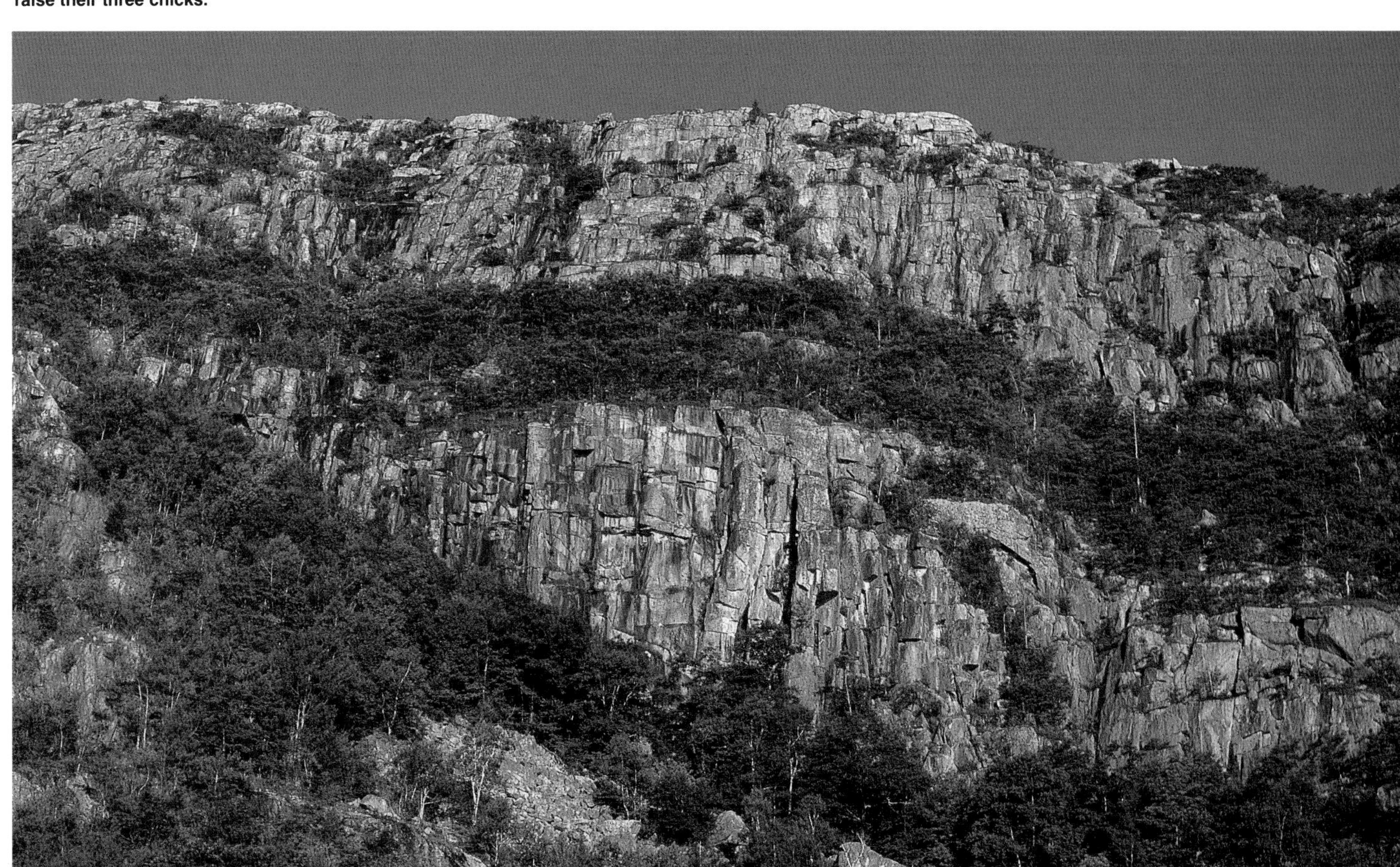

Point. While the repair work went on, he explored the island and chose the name, *L'Isle des Monts Deserts* (island of the barren mountains), simply because it was descriptive.

Demonstrably, it was a good description, because, as we reached the top of Cadillac, we could see we were atop a bare granite dome similar to the other mountains of the island—Champlain, Dorr, Sargent, and Bald Peak among them.

Slightly less tall at 1,270 feet, Dorr Mountain was named for George Bucknam Dorr, the visionary behind Acadia National Park. Dorr, together with Dr. Charles W. Eliot, president of Harvard, were public-minded men with wealthy friends who saw the threat to the island from lumbermen and developers as intolerable. Aided by a gift of eleven thousand acres from John D. Rockefeller, they raised enough money to buy the rest of the land, which they donated to the government in 1919 as a park. President Woodrow Wilson appointed Dorr the first superintendent at a salary of one dollar a month. Today this forty thousand-acre landscape of scenic wonder is the second most-visited national park in the United States.

The view from the summit even before sunrise was truly spectacular. Looking around Dicken remarked, "People are always telling me, 'Go to Africa!' 'Go to Asia!' 'Go to South America, you'd love it!' Being here makes me say, '*Why?*' "

Dicken and I walked from the car to an enormous mound of granite and sat down to wait for the sunrise.

Maybe I am a jaded traveler but one of my pet peeves is this: Having, at the end of a long, tiring overseas flight, the entire planeload of passengers applaud when the wheels touch American soil. This is not an issue of patriotism; it is just something I have always found annoying. The moment the sun rose out of the sea that morning, fully a thousand people scattered over the crown of Cadillac Mountain broke into spontaneous applause. Instead of being annoyed, I got goosebumps. It was that kind of place.

Behind me, two late arrivals, a son urging his father along, reached a spot where they could see the breathtaking 360-degree view and the orange fireball to the east. The boy was about seven and wore a St. Louis Padres baseball cap. Unlike some of the other children who had been forced out of bed too early, this boy's face was alive with awe. In a breathless voice he said, "Geesh, Dad, who *built* this place?"

In a quieter tone of voice his father replied, "God, son."

After a while the early birds started to drift back to their cars, but we did not. As we looked around, I asked Dicken, who is a keen student of geology, to explain something of the geologic origins of Maine. It was an ideal vantage point at which to ask the question. We could see many miles, both inland, up and down the coast, and far out to sea. Those "precious isles set in a silver sea," as Maine poet Celia Leighton Thaxter once put it, stretched out before us like a pearl necklace as far as the eye could see.

"Eons and eons ago, the coast of Maine didn't look like this at all," Dicken began.

"According to geologists, time and the elements eroded ancient mountains

The view from Cadillac Mountain, Mt. Desert Island.

leaving a thick deposit of sediments in an equally ancient ocean basin. Hot molten granite then rose up like blobs in a lava lamp through thousands of feet of sedimentary rock, never actually reaching the surface. As it cooled, huge chunks of these deposits collapsed into the magma. Deep below the surface the roots of a massive mountain range were forming. Over some hundreds of millions of years, the forces of nature eroded these new mountain ranges, which were comparable in scale to the Alps or the Himalayas, nearly flat. And that formed a low coastal plain of marshes and beaches."

It occurred to me, as Dicken was talking, that in that prehistoric era, had there been anyone to look, they would have seen a rather undistinguished looking Maine Coast with none of the dramatic geological elements that make the present-day coast and islands such a delightful area in which to cruise.

"But *that,*" Dicken continued dramatically, "was before the ice came. The glacier of ice that sat on top of the world like a crystal crown grew larger and larger. It expanded southward across Maine and eventually all of New England. They say that it was a mile thick above the highest point in Maine; its weight was unimaginable. The ice sheet swept out into the Atlantic more than three hundred miles to the continental shelf. The land beneath was gouged and scraped. The hills, marshland, and beaches easily gave way, allowing the glaciers to carve into the mountain range's roots below, sculpting the hard granite. Soon, geologically speaking, the ice began to melt. As it did, the material that had been pushed and dragged by the glacier became places like Cape Cod, Martha's Vineyard, and Nantucket.

"The sea level rose, and Maine's former coastal plain was flooded. The higher parts of that plain are now the fishing banks off the present coast—the Georges Bank and the Grand Bank. The sea swept inland to where we are now. Ocean waters and melted ice drowned the former gouges, gorges, and trenches formed by the glacier, and they became estuaries and bays. Somes Sound, over there, was also created; it is the only fjord on the east coast of the United States. Most of the green-clad islands you can see from here, including the one you're standing on, are the remnants of the resistant granite roots of the long gone mountains."

Geologists call this a "drowned coast," a term I never fully understood until Dicken explained it to me. The down easters call this part of their world the "bold coast." From our vantage atop Cadillac Mountain I could now see quite clearly the aptness of both.

One of the results of all this geological turmoil was that a coastline, which probably had not exceeded 250 miles in its former incarnation was now so irregular and indented that it measures over 2,500 miles long. (It is still only 236 miles as the sea gull flies.)

Another result—to my mind a more astonishing one—is the fact that there are more islands in the Maine Archipelago than there are in the Caribbean, more than on the Dalmatian Coast of the Adriatic, more even than in all of Polynesia, that vast expanse of Oceania stretching from New Zealand, north to Hawaii, and east to Easter Island.

Ten

ONE OF THEM LOCAL YAHOOS

For the first time since the fog had trapped us in Corea we were again prisoners of the weather. Not fog this time, but rain. The showers started and stopped and, like a record with a stuck needle, the cycle repeated itself for two days.

At times the rain was heavy, forcing us to sit resentfully below decks. Since we were determined to explore more of Mount Desert Island, however, we waited. We had yet to see the famous Otter Cliffs, Thunder Hole, Jordan Pond, Seal Harbor, Somesville, the Wild Gardens of Acadia, or any of the fifty miles of carriage trails John D. Rockefeller had commissioned.

During one of the lulls in the rain, we moved up to the cockpit. Betsy, who is a card-carrying member of the Defenders of Wildlife, instituted what she called the Friday Afternoon Duck Races. Tossing bits of bread over the side, she and

Betsy feeds the black ducks in Northeast Harbor.

Eliza attracted scores of black ducks. It was extraordinary how word among the birds spread. How did they know so quickly? Like water rushing into a drain, they materialized from every corner of Northeast Harbor to surround the boat and compete for dinner. Eliza tried conscientiously to be fair to the less aggressive ones and especially to a lone sea gull, who was trying his damnedest to poach.

Early the following morning under clear skies we stood on the precipice of Otter Cliffs. One hundred feet below, breakers pummeled the rugged escarpment. Black guillemots, tiny members of the auk family, darted in and out of crevices where they lay their eggs on the bare rock. These alcids, like their relatives, the razorbills and puffins, are expert diving hunters. Underwater they use their wings as fins in their pursuit of red rock eels, their favorite prey. Why the inside of a guillemot's mouth and a red rock eel are *exactly* the same color—a showy scarlet—is a riddle no expert seems able to unravel.

Along the corniche road above the cliffs we chanced upon a middle-aged woman who was quite excited. She pointed to white water off Otter Point, and declared, feverishly, in an authentic Maine accent, "There's a hunchback whale! There's a hunchback whale! I read about it in the Ellsworth paper. It's been coming closer to shore than ever. See it's blowing now."

Eliza, Betsy, Dicken, and I eagerly scanned the waters off the cliff-lined point and, sure enough, the water was breaking. We had been so anxious to spot a whale on our trip that seeing one so close to shore was sufficiently thrilling to ignore what seemed like an extraordinary mistake for a Mainer to make, to wit, calling a *humpback* a *hunchback*.

While we stared at this crashing spectacle, the hunchback whale lady moved on to the next group of tourists. In the distance we heard her saying, look, there's a hunchback whale. After a little more staring, Betsy said almost to herself, "Wait a second . . ." Then, at the same moment that I realized we were staring at water breaking on a ledge, I heard Dicken say, "Wait a second, that's not a whale. That's a *rock*."

We looked around, but the hunchback whale lady was nowhere to be seen. Most likely she was around the next bend cackling over the sheer delight of having hoodwinked another group of brainless tourists.

On the way back to *Consolation* we stopped at Sieur de Monts where the Bar Harbor Garden Club maintains the Wild Gardens of Acadia. More than four hundred species of heaths, ferns, berries, shrubs, trees, and wildflowers are planted in the twelve different habitats that are found in the wild on Mount Desert Island. It is an impressive endeavor, of which the Garden Club must be proud. On leaving I passed a couple who were speaking in the telltale accent of the Bronx, a borough of my native New York City. I overheard the woman say to the man, "Plants don't really do that much for me."

Between the Hunchback Whale Lady and this Philistine, I thought to myself, maybe it was time to mosey on.

We made straight for the rounded rock beaches of Baker Island four miles southeast of Mount Desert. Baker has no sheltered harbor, but the day was calm. We anchored on the north side of the island. *Consolation* takes a little while to

Somesville: Tending pink petunias and red geraniums in a unique wall garden.

Bass Harbor Head Light at the southern tip of Mount Desert Island.

settle down after anchoring; all boats have their idiosyncrasies, and this is one of hers. She is like a racehorse, impatient, undecided, pawing the turf, shifting from side to side against her halter. Often, even after she calms down, she will lie just a little differently than other boats moored nearby. That morning our only neighbors were lobster pots, and sure enough when *Consolation* stopped her shenanigans we were lying athwart some guy's potwarp. Betsy volunteered to stay aboard; she would be able to pull *Consolation* forward on her anchor in case the lobsterman arrived.

One-half of Baker is privately owned; the other half is part of Acadia National Park. It is no accident that Charles W. Eliot, who was one of the driving forces behind Acadia, became interested in nearby Baker Island and specifically in the family who first inhabited it.

In 1899 while still president of Harvard College, Eliot wrote a book called *John Gilley, One of the Forgotten Millions.* It was a slim volume and an unusual endeavor in that or any other time, because it memorialized the life and times of a "common" man. "With the rarest exceptions," Eliot wrote at the beginning of the book, "the death of each human individual is followed in a short time by

The Thaddeus Shepley Somes Memorial Bridge is in Somesville, the village that caps Somes Sound, the only fjord on the east coast of the United States.

At Sieur de Monts the Bar Harbor Garden Club maintains the Wild Gardens of Acadia.

complete oblivion." Eliot's book about John Gilley formulated that rare exception.

As I sat on a grassy bluff dotted with huckleberries, I read from Eliot's book. Surrounding me were eight or nine worn gravestones bleached a glowing white by generations of sunshine. In the distance were the mountains of Mount Desert. Each headstone bore the name Gilley, and I quickly became lost in time as I read about William and Hannah Gilley, their twelve children (of whom John was the third), and their fifty-eight grandchildren.

The cemetery on a bluff on Baker Island faces the plutonic domes of Mount Desert Island. There, I read from Charles Eliot's book, *John Gilley, One of the Forgotten Millions:* "With the rarest excèptions," he wrote, "the death of each human individual is followed in a short time by complete oblivion."

"Forest and sea shaped their world; farming, fishing, and hunting sustained them. They worked hard. Callused hands wielded an ax, guided a plow, trimmed a sail, treadled a spinning wheel or held a child. To their skilled labor, the land produced vegetables, forage for stock and a little wheat. They caught herring and mackerel and picked up lobsters in the shallows. Like us they knew joy and sorrow, labor and rest, adversity and success."

At the point in John Gilley's life when adversity had indeed given way to success and when, by prevailing standards, he had become financially quite comfortable, an accident at sea ended it all. Halfway between Bear and Sutton Islands, Gilley's skiff foundered under the surge of a rogue wave.

Eliot wrote: ". . . but the old man, chilled by the cold water and stunned by the waves, which beat about his head, had lost his hold and sunk into the sea. In half an hour John Gilley had passed from a hearty and successful old age in this world . . . into the voiceless mystery of death. No trace of his body was ever found. It disappeared into the waters on which he had played and worked as boy and man all his long and fortunate life. He left his family well provided for, and full of gratitude and praise for his honorable career and his sterling character."

What finer epitaph could a man ask for?

Thus spiritually reinvigorated by tales of the Gilleys, I returned to *Consolation,* where Betsy was having what looked like a set-to with an angry lobsterman. I assumed he owned the trap over which we were anchored. Worried, I rowed quickly toward the boat.

We had tried not to run afoul of working fishermen during our trip. They deserve respect for their courage and skill and for the hard lives they lead. I have seen cruising sailboats, insisting on their sail-over-power right-of-way, plow straight across the path of a working lobster boat. Having witnessed such idiocy, I wonder why there is not universal animosity on the part of the lobstermen toward vacationing yachtsmen. Remarkably, as we had discovered, the reverse is true: The sailor who shows respect for the hardworking lobsterman is nearly always rewarded in kind.

Today we seemed to be at fault, and I hastened to make amends. By the time I got back to *Consolation,* however, he had roared off in a blare of diesel exhaust and badly amplified rock music.

"What'd he say?" I asked Betsy. "He seemed pissed."

"That's what I thought! He was yelling at me, and I couldn't for the life of me hear what he was saying over that music! I kept saying, 'Don't worry, I'll move.' And he just kept yelling at me."

I made *Hoggie*'s painter fast and clambered aboard.

"So finally the guy must've realized I couldn't hear a word," Betsy continued. "But when he turned down his radio, I felt like such a fool. The whole time I thought he was complaining, he was complimenting *Consolation.* Saying how beautiful he thought she was and asking what kind of wood her planking is. It wasn't even his lobster pot."

It seemed like as good a time as any to shove off, lest the real owner of the pot materialize. And that is what we did.

In the same way that the Porcupine Islands seem to defend Bar Harbor, the miniature archipelago of the Cranberry Islands—Great Cranberry, Little Cranberry, Sutton, and Baker—plug the entrance to Somes Sound. The berries, which gave the archipelago its name, are long gone from the islands . . . not so the mosquitoes (a drainage program undertaken in the 1920s failed).

Islesford is the settlement on the west side of Little Cranberry. The Islesford Historical Museum, which dominates the wharf area, features exhibits of early Acadian history. In the entrance hall there is a rowboat that caught my eye. "Built by Chummy Spurling on Little Cranberry," the sign said. Damn if it didn't look familiar! It certainly did, and Dicken confirmed it. Chummy's skiff was the wooden "plug" on which *Hog Wild* was based. Jarvis Newman across the way in Southwest Harbor had built *Hoggie* in Fiberglas to the specifications of Chummy Spurling's original, commodious design.

The view from the steps of the museum was of Hadlock Cove. *Consolation* lay moored among a fleet of lobster boats with distinctive triangular "riding sails," which fly from small, mizzen-like masts off their sterns. The whole fleet had them—sewn from canvas, dyed bold shades of red, blue, and green. Some fishing harbors adopt these stabilizing sails, most do not. Lobstermen are not known for sheep-like tendencies, but in this regard there is an exception. Either the whole fleet is thus equipped, or, inexplicably, it is not.

No matter the reason, the colorful sails enhanced an already picturesque sight as we watched the orange sun backlight Spurling Point in the distance. We decided to take a walk before darkness fell. An amiable passerby encouraged us to

Dartmouth Professor Emeritus Ashley Bryan has been painting on the Cranberries since 1946.

visit Helen Ham's flower garden. It was worth the short trip. Shell pink roses peeked through a moss-covered split-rail fence. Above the high enclosure stood delphiniums, some five, even six feet tall. They were blue-violet. White and pink foxgloves completed the picture.

In any light the garden would have been outstanding; seen in the golden light of that July afternoon, it was exquisite. I wanted to thank Ms. Ham, but a discreet sign on the walk to the house said Private. I imagined a gentle soul behind such a delicate garden, and nothing would have induced me to violate her wish.

We headed back toward the harbor with the intention of treating ourselves to a rare meal ashore. On the way I busied myself photographically, taking advantage of the late light. Betsy, Dicken, and Eliza strolled ahead stopping to talk to a man repairing lobster pots in his yard. When I caught up, Betsy introduced me to Arthur Fernald, the lobsterman she thought had been yelling at her for anchoring on top of his buoy off Baker Island.

Arthur could not have been farther from the yelling sort. Soft-spoken and thoughtful, he wears a hearing aid (which might have accounted for some of the earlier hollering and misunderstanding), and his eyeglass lenses are of a thickness that divides the line of the temples the way a camera's split-image rangefinder does. Arthur's muttonchops connect with the ends of his mustaches, giving him a somewhat anachronistic appearance. But his outfit of blue jeans, a checkered western-style shirt with snap buttons, and a red baseball cap sporting the legend "Shoreline Trap 207-273-3865" placed him squarely in the present.

We invited Arthur to join us for a beer. "Terrific," Arthur replied, "I'll tell my wife, Ann. We'll join you at, say, six, six-thirty at Puddles." When he mentioned the name of the local tourist watering hole, I must have inadvertently grimaced, because he said with a wink, "Name like that makes ya want to puke, doesn't it?"

The Islesford Congregational Church, Little Cranberry Island.

As we wandered back to the harbor, Betsy remarked to Dicken how lucky we were to be sailing on a boat as pretty as *Consolation.* She was the vehicle upon which so many of our chance encounters had depended and was, after all, how we had met Arthur Fernald.

Puddles was a pleasant enough, if over-priced, bar/restaurant catering to day-trippers from Northeast and Southwest harbors. And Arthur was right: The name was, as the English say, too cute by half, loathsome enough to be lumped together with the Dew Drop Inn and the Nick Nack Nook. We sat at a table for six, mollified by the first sip of ice-cold beer, and the conversation soon drifted to relations between the locals and those from away. Ann told us that Little Cranberry has one hundred year-round residents, but that the summerfolk, whom she laughingly calls "summer complaints," swell the population to three hundred. And that does not count the procession of ferry boats making daily round trips from Mount Desert.

Arthur Fernald.

She told us that when she worked at the Islesford Historical Museum visitors would often come in to ask her questions about life on Little Cranberry. "Really I never minded," she explained. "In a way it was part of my job at the museum, but for some reason they would always get around to saying something like, 'How on earth can you live here all year round? I mean, *what do you do all winter?*' "

"Can you believe how rude people can be?" Arthur put in.

"I always wanted to get up the nerve to answer, 'Trying to get up the energy to deal with you summer people,' but I never did."

Warming to the subject, Arthur continued, "Why just t'other day I was driving my truck uptown, and there were these turkeys walking six abreast in the middle of the road. I downshifted. Then I had to put on my brakes until I was creeping along about five miles an hour. Finally one of them looked back at me, and I could tell by the look on his face that he was thinking, 'Look, there's one of them local yahoos driving along at five miles an hour.' "

"About the thirty-first of July," Arthur concluded wearily, "I start looking forward to Labor Day."

Early the next morning there was a rap-rapping on the hull. I climbed the companionway ladder into the cockpit. Alongside in a little skiff, Arthur and Ann sat smiling. "We brought you these." Ann handed me a plate of muffins, warm from the oven. "They're made with strawberries and rhubarb fresh from my garden." We shared the just-brewed coffee and had a breakfast feast.

Arthur was dying to get a closer look at *Consolation.* Dicken showed him below. He looked her over with the practiced eye of a professional, occasionally thumping on a beam here and a plank there. Satisfied by the solid sounds his knocking produced, he pronounced her fit.

On the saloon table I happened to have a copy of a picture book about wooden boats called *Wood, Water, and Light.* When Arthur spotted it, his eyes lit up. He immediately flipped to page thirty. There in the lobster boat chapter, he proudly showed us two photographs of his own boat *Sea Chimes.*

"I just put five fresh coats of paint on her," Arthur said proudly.

Arthur's beloved *Sea Chimes*.

"Five?"

"Oh, yeah, you've got to have at least five just to get her topsides nice and smooth. She's right behind you, you know." Arthur pointed to the boat we'd seen the day before.

Sea Chimes' topsides were like glass, as it happens, and painted a royal blue. Her rub rail and deck was sand, or pongee-colored; her trunk cabin was white on the sides, and on the horizontal surfaces it was painted a color I call Caribbean green. The care Arthur Fernald put into *Sea Chimes,* which, don't forget, is a working boat subject to the wear and tear of a brutal climate and the knockabout business of lobstering, was evident in every detail. It was fun to admire her in the pictures and at the same time *in vita*—moored as she was not twenty yards away.

I struggled to find something appropriate to say that would show Arthur how appreciative I was of his efforts to make *Sea Chimes* the prettiest lobster boat *I* had ever seen. Like the proverbial comic strip light bulb, inspiration came to me in a flash.

"Arthur," I said, "would you be willing to autograph the book for me?"

Judging by the expression on Arthur's face, I'd said the right thing. Before we said good-bye, he wrote in the margin next to the photograph of his beloved *Sea Chimes:* "The Very Best of Wishes to Betsy Eliza Dicken & Chris—Arthur Fernald."

Eleven
THE MOST VOLUPTUOUS ROCKS

LUNT IS THE NAME TO HAVE if you live in the tiny village of Frenchboro (population 43) on one of Maine's twelve Long Islands. This particular Long Island is the one dominated by Lunt Harbor. At the head of the harbor is a lone wharf. The lobster pound is there, managed by Dave Lunt, president of Lunt &

Lunt, and you can buy a terrific lobster roll at Lunt's Dockside Deli. They sell Lunt & Lunt sweatshirts and baseball hats. As often as not Sanford Lunt can be found on the fuel dock weighing in the lobstermen's catches; he is Dave's father. Seventy-seven-year-old Cecil Lunt wanders down each morning to check out the comings and goings from his favorite spot, the bench in front of the Lunt & Lunt office. Cecil is Sanford's brother.

A sign behind Cecil's bench reads:

DOCKSIDE DELI
LUNT & LUNT

MOORINGS LOBSTERS
GAS FOOD

A second sign advertises: Take Home a Souvenir Organic Mussel Earring. $3.00 a pair. One suspects that the Lunts have figured out that *organic* is one of those words people who own sailboats like. A third sign touts other services they provide for visiting yachtsmen, proving that the Lunts leave no economic stone unturned: Moorings $10.00 a Night, Garbage $1.00 a Bag. Yet another sign di-

Lunt Harbor, Frenchboro, Long Island.

The Lunt brothers, Sanford and Cecil.

rects the visitor down the hill to Becky's Boutique. You guessed it, Becky is Mrs. Rebecca Lunt. I did something at Becky's Boutique I don't usually do: I bought a T-shirt, the proceeds from which sale, I was assured by Becky herself, went in aid of the Frenchboro Volunteer Fire Department. The instant I saw it I knew it had to be mine. In fire-engine-red letters it said: "Frenchboro Fire Department. You Light 'Em. We Fight 'Em."

Thrilled with my purchase, I wandered back to Lunt's wharf. Inside the office, Sanford Lunt watched while his son Dave was going over the receipts with his grandson Dave, Jr., who, one assumes, is heir apparent to the Lunt Fortune.

I pull the collective leg of the Lunts because they were so unabashed about their commercialism, but actually life is pretty tough in little Frenchboro. Beside the Dockside Deli and Becky's Boutique there are no stores in Frenchboro, not even a market. A trip to the supermarket means an eighteen-mile round-trip by water, if you have your own boat. If you don't, there is a twice-a-week ferry. You have to go to Bass Harbor on the Wednesday ferry, shop, spend the night at the Colonial (the special rate for islanders is $38), and return to Frenchboro on Thursday's ferry.

The Frenchboro School has thirteen students, nine grades, one room, and one teacher. After Frenchboro, the children must board with a family in Southwest Harbor if they want to attend high school. Such hardships have driven most of the young people from the island. To stem the depopulation a group of islanders founded the Frenchboro Future Development Corporation.

With assistance from Maine State Housing, a gift of land from the Rockefellers (who own much of unspoiled Long Island), and donations by islanders, the FFDC built six houses and advertised for modern-day homesteaders to live in them. Sue Sylvester and her husband Joe were among the first applicants. With directions from a Lunt grandson, Eliza and I walked up the dusty road the town of Frenchboro had built as their contribution to the homesteading project. Sue's house is a one-and-a-half story structure, stained gray with white trim. Above the door is a carved wooden eagle; its beak holds a streamer, which reads "Don't Give Up the Ship."

That first winter, homesteader Sue Sylvester's father mailed her a poem called *"Don't Quit!"*

A boy about six greeted us as we approached the house. He did so with the friendliness of a Labrador puppy. Patrick yelled for his mom, and a pretty blond woman, tan and fit looking, emerged. Her smile was as engaging and welcoming as her son's.

While Patrick and Eliza played on the Sylvester's swing (there is nothing quite like the speed with which a friendship can develop between an only child stuck on a sailboat and a child who lives on a remote island with forty-three residents), Sue told me about her experiences as a latter-day homesteader.

"We wouldn't own a house like this were it not for the corporation," Sue said. "We couldn't have afforded anything like this at home."

Home was Marblehead, Massachusetts, where Joe was a lobsterman. Sue and Joe were high school sweethearts who married right after graduation. Business was bad for Joe, and Sue had her hands full with Patrick and his younger brother, Sean. When Sue heard about the homesteading program on TV, she immediately added her name to a long list of applicants. Interviews with the Frenchboro Future Development Corporation followed. They were looking for emotionally stable families with a means of income compatible with the economic peculiarities of island life; writing, painting, and, of course, fishing were among the "acceptable" occupations. After the culling process, six families were chosen, and Sue's was among them. Each family put a deposit down on a lot, and the FFDC began building the houses. The deal was simple and affordable: a modest down payment, three years of renting, and in the end an option to buy.

Now four years later three houses stand empty. The difficulties of eking out a living as an independent lobsterman were factors in each of the three families' decisions to leave.

"You've got to be tough to hack it come winter," Sue told me. The first ten months in Frenchboro she spent alone while her husband was waiting for his Maine lobster license (he continued to fish in Marblehead). "We moved in three days after Christmas in a raging blizzard. I was so lonely that winter. People from home would call, and I'd go mental on them. I love Joey, and I missed him something fierce . . . and of course I worried about him while he was out fishing."

Looking skyward at the gorgeous July day, clear and sunny, Sue said, "It's hard to imagine how tough it really is here during the winter."

That first winter her father mailed her a poem called "Don't Quit!."

"I kept it Scotch-taped to my mirror and often looked at it. Sometimes I really think of myself as a pioneer. I didn't quit, and I don't intend to now. But, you know, in the end I'm afraid this island will die out. There are a lot of old people, and few of the young ones are willing to stay here. At the beginning of the program, there were lists and lists of applicants. Now the project is begging people to homestead. Truthfully," she tapered off sadly, "the program is struggling."

As we sailed out of Lunt Harbor later that day we passed the brand new fishing pens, which Mariculture, an Ellsworth company, had recently installed. There were 325,000 Donaldson sea trout fattening up within them, and Sue Sylvester has recently been hired to feed them. We looked in vain to give this inspirational woman a wave and a good luck as we passed, but she was nowhere to be seen.

We sneaked into Burnt Coat Harbor on Swans Island by the back door—a narrow, curvy passage between Harbor Island and Stanley Point. It was late after-

noon. On a broad reach and a fair tide the short hop from Frenchboro had been as pleasant a sail as one could want.

We found an anchoring spot a short distance west of the rest of the fleet. I was thinking of the next morning's photography. Burnt Coat looked like a busy working harbor. By anchoring on the far side I would have a fine vantage point from which to shoot the early morning harbor bustle.

Betsy and Eliza repaired to the galley where they began preparing homemade pizza—a *Consolation* first. Dicken went forward to practice playing his plastic, 100 percent seaworthy, ocean-going guitar. No one knows where Dicken finds such things. And I busied myself in the cockpit, catching up on my journal via the miracle of my Toshiba lap computer, which Fitz had direct-wired to *Consolation*'s battery bank.

The early morning activity at Burnt Coat was every bit as bustling as I

Burnt Coat, Swans Island.

expected—and as beautiful. The sun turned everything golden. On *Consolation*'s bow I photographed what I realized was an archetypal working harbor scene, the epicenter of Maine coastal village life.

Skiffs laden with repaired traps or buckets of bait or newly-painted buoys motored out to lobster boats, their drivers standing astern holding the steering arms of their outboards in their fingers. Everywhere I could hear the deep-throated growl of well-tuned diesel engines roaring to early morning life. One by one the lobster boats would ease up to the fuel dock, the next one replacing the replenished one in an effortless, unvarying ballet choreographed generations before. Before the sun was completely above the ridge, the last of the lobster boats filed out of the harbor, chugged around the Hockamock Head Lighthouse, and disappeared for the day's work.

Meanwhile, aboard *Consolation,* a far less strenuous morning was unfolding. Eliza and Betsy remained cozy in their berths, I considered my plan-of-the-day (at a leisurely pace), and Dicken was preparing for his daily ablution.

A nice thing about Dicken is the way he keeps his morning swim a personal experience. I'm too much of a wuss to go swimming in 68-degree water, let alone

Skiffs laden with repaired traps or buckets of bait or newly-painted buoys motored out to lobster boats, their drivers standing astern holding the steering arms of their outboards in their fingers.

the 46-degree water Dicken swam in off Campobello Island. But, setting that aside, most cold-water swimmers I've sailed with seem to have an insurmountable need to badger others into swimming with them. To Dicken's credit, not so he. He simply gets out of his bunk, grabs his towel, and after liberal applications of Dr. Bronner's Castile Liquid Soap—a ritual process he calls Bronnerizing—he dives alone into the bone-chilling waters of the Gulf of Maine.

After breakfast Eliza and I set off to explore Burnt Coat and to discover why it came to be called *Burnt Coat.* Thanks to Norman Burns, we did.

Seventy-four-year-old Norman Burns was working on his lobster boat, the *Pamela Jean.* He had her hauled out of the water. With a paint brush in one hand and white paint splatter all over his brown trousers, blue checked shirt, and even his red hat, he said, "I don't really do much lobstering anymore, but I do like to keep my hand in. Touch her up now and again. Keep her shipshape." Four remaining lower teeth gave him the appearance of an English bulldog, but there was nothing pugnacious about his personality.

Eliza asked him forthrightly why his town had such a weird name. Mr. Burns gave her a dazzling four-toothed grin and said, "Well, I'll tell ya. The whole island used to be called Burnt Coat. That was before they named it Swans. This French explorer Champlain stopped here in 1604. There must have been a big forest fire before he came because he called the island *Brûlée Côte,* which is French for *burnt coast.* When the English came, they couldn't pronounce that. So they called it Burnt Coat instead."

Eliza followed this explanation with wide-eyed attention.

"You seem like a smart girl, Eliza," Burns said. His face took on a distracted, far-away look. "I have a daughter, too. Course she's a lot older than you. I named my boat after her. Pamela Jean's her name, but she was never quite right. Fact is, she's retarded."

He proceeded to tell us his daughter's story with a startling directness. "Moment she was born, she started to have convulsions. We took her to every damn hospital in the state, but they just shook their heads and said, 'Let her go.' Still alive, you know, but I don't have to pay for her any more. I used to. I wanted to. But now the state does, so that's all right. Sad, though, she doesn't even know who we are."

"But I can't complain," he resumed after a pause. "I've been married forty-seven happy years, my other daughter lives right over there, next door to us, and my grandchildren, well, they're just great."

As often happens when Eliza is around, the mood quickly shifted.

"Look!" she shouted. Swimming past Norman Burns's dock in close formation were two pairs of birds: a goose couple and a mallard couple. They were paddling along together as happy as can be, and they looked like they were on a double date.

"They're mine," Burns said. "The four of them've been glued at the hip since I got 'em. You should see the gander if something bothers those ducks, why he'll go nuts trying to protect them. Damnedest thing *I've* seen in seventy-four years!"

The sail to Blue Hill would be an all-day affair, a thirty-mile trip. We resolved to get an early start and the next morning left Burnt Coat in the lobstermen's procession.

On the way out we passed a run-down dogger of a boat that Fitz would have called the *H.M.S. Grotesque.* She was a catamaran, whose designer had accomplished what I would have thought would have been impossible: He designed a sailboat to look exactly like a 1957 Cadillac.

To make matters worse she had one of the all-time worst boat names I've ever spotted. She was called *Sea-yuh!.* Maybe I'm old-fashioned, but I have an aversion to boats with *sea*-related puns in their names. I base this on the most personal of experiences. Twice I have crossed oceans on a ketch called *Sealestial.* Although there is a special place in my heart for *Sealestial* (not least because she saw me safely across two oceans), her name makes me cringe.

Since leaving Essex, we have spotted more than our share of nastily-named boats. *C-Venture* from Vero Beach, Florida, is one that springs to mind. And *Gypsea.* And, ugh, *Frequensea III.*

We have passed boats named *Centerfold* and *Bottom Snatcher, Charged It* and *She's Worth It, Able Mable* and *Carrie & Grant.*

The competition became so stiff that Dicken, Betsy, and I decided to hold an election for the title, "Most Loathsome Boat Name." *Sea-Yuh!* won hands-down, but *Dunwishin'* and *Wright A'Weigh* came in closely tied for second.

A midmorning visit to Buckle Island.

Harbor seals bask on a half-tide ledge in Blue Hill Bay.

Midmorning we paid a brief visit to Buckle Island, a gem of an island off the northwest point of Swans. Buckle has beaches with the most voluptuous rocks imaginable to a photographer's eye.

As we nosed up to the leeward shore, Dicken, who is constantly on the lookout for trends, had an inspirational flash. Just as the higher prows of the "Novies" gave way to the lower, more subtle sheers of the Beal's Island lobster boats, Dicken observed that, as we sail westward, the higher cliffs are giving way to more sensuous, granity, rolling rocks like those on the beach at Buckle.

After too short a stop we passed out of Jericho Bay across the Casco Passage and into Blue Hill Bay. A ledge to starboard was bursting with seals basking in the midday sun. They looked like sausages browning in a skillet. When one of them would roll over, I could imagine a giant invisible fork turning the sausages until they were nice and crispy.

I was reminded of a Gary Larson cartoon. Two sharks, heads out of the water,

are looking at a man sunbathing on a raft. One shark says to the other, "I can never tell when they're done."

A little further along, another ledge was chock full of cormorants. Because they have no oil glands these seabirds are forced to air-dry their wings by holding them outstretched and motionless. The effect of a line of somber-looking cormorants doing this reminds one of gargoyles on a gothic cathedral. Because they are black and have a rather sinister appearance, they look like they belong in a Charles Addams' cartoon.

Although they are now protected, cormorants were nearly eradicated by angry fishermen. Shags, as the fishermen call them when they are being nice, attack herring-filled weirs causing panic among the fish and death even to those the shags don't catch. When the fishermen are really provoked by the cormorants (as when they gorge on baby salmon), they use the meanest moniker they can muster. They call them *lawyer birds.*

We passed between Mount Desert and Bartlett Island (also owned by Peggy and David Rockefeller). They bought Bartlett in 1973 to rescue it from developers. One wonders what coastal Maine would now be like had it not been for the benign intervention of that powerful family.

By late afternoon we'd reached Closson Point, Morgan Bay, just a few road miles from Blue Hill Harbor. Friends of the Cranes' and of Betsy's live there in a compound of cabins called Tall Timbers. In true cruising yachtsman style, we paid them an unannounced visit and were promptly rewarded with an invitation for dinner.

Built in the 1920s, Tall Timbers is a collection of half-a-dozen log cabins. Of rustic design—almost with an Adirondack feeling—they have fieldstone fireplaces and deeply shaded porches, each with a sea view. The cabins are supported by pilings built right on top of the bedrock. The sixteen grandparents, children, and grandchildren in the family can occupy different ones. That and a mile-long driveway affords them the maximum in old-style privacy. A larger, central cabin contains the kitchen and common dining room as well as the biggest verandah with a sublime view of the bay.

Barbara Priester Deely, daughter of the man who bought it, told me that although she considers herself reclusive ("We've got everything here. What more could we possibly want?"), she has a friend—a forty-year summer resident of Blue Hill—whose recluseness extends to a firm refusal of every cocktail party invitation she has ever received.

Barbara imitated the friend's voice and manner, " 'Oh,' she says, 'thank you *so* much for inviting me, but I'd rather not come.' "

Before dinner Betsy and I borrowed a car (our mooching tendencies knew no limit) and drove to Blue Hill for sunset pictures. We climbed the hill, which is renowned for its spectacular 360-degree views. Had I known the trek up a dry stream bed would be as rigorous as it was, I would have stayed at Tall Timbers

---

Jim Deely enjoys the quiet of a still morning at Tall Timbers, Morgan Bay.

Skipping down Main Street past the Water Witch: The village of Castine at the upper reach of Penobscot Bay.

Two beauties in Brooksville: Not a typical Maine coastal scene.

Moose Island, Blue Hill Bay. West of Mount Desert.

sipping a martini. Still, the view was, to use Eliza's word, awesome. We could see Blue Hill Harbor and Bay, the Bagaduce River, the Penobscot River and Bay, as well as First Pond, Second Pond, Third Pond, and Fourth Pond.

Remember George and Bush Islands? At the top of the forest warden's tower on Blue Hill I thought briefly of the former First Lady. Due south of the tower I could just barely make out Mother Bush Pond.

Twelve

"BOMBASTO FURIOSO"

IF I SEEM OBSESSED with pond names, island names, boat names, any-kind-of-names, perhaps I am. But where else beside Maine could you find a safe anchorage in between three islands named Bold, Devil, and Hell's Half Acre?

Below the Deer Island Thorofare, which connects Jericho and East Penobscot Bays, lies an archipelago called Merchants Row. One would be hard pressed to find a cruising ground more enchanting than this anywhere in the world. Thirty-three islands strung along a several mile stretch make for an abundance of secret anchorages and hideaway gunkholes. Densely wooded, with white granite shores, the islands of Merchant Row are numerous enough to afford solitary nature walks even though nearby Deer Island Thorofare is one of the busiest marine passages on the coast.

We spent a warm July night in the lee of Hell's Half Acre at the eastern end of Merchants Row. We dined on halibut and listened to the radio after dinner. The lights of Stonington were dimly visible two miles to the east, but it was otherwise silent and dark. We would head for Stonington the next morning, a virtual metropolis by Devil Island standards, but for the moment we were alone.

Someone once said that if you wanted to find a Maine fishing village more genuine than Stonington you had better look in Canada. From the Thorofare the view of town is dominated by a tangle of wharves, jetties, docks, piers, and landings crowding every foot of waterfront. The backs of most of the buildings stick out over the water, supported by pilings; below are floats and rafts for skiffs. White and red seem to be the preference in paint colors. There are chandleries, bait shacks, lobstermen's co-ops, fishermen's co-ops, packing plants, derricks on barges, and even a retail fish market or two. Behind the waterfront row of buildings is a hill, Green Head; the center of Stonington's residential area is the four tiers of houses on the side of this hill.

We anchored between *Ms. Peggy II* and a dragger called *Sea Flea IV.* There were a handful of pleasure boats in the harbor but only three other sailboats beside *Consolation.* Stonington is a no-nonsense working port, make no mistake. This is not to say that it is grubby or ugly. Far from it, Stonington is a village of stately shade trees and a riotous mishmash of architectural styles: clapboard colonials, shingle-style houses weathered to a silvery gray, and even a couple of mansard-roofed Victorians.

Stonington, Deer Isle.

I was anxious to get ashore. After routine ship's work—furling the main, coiling sheets, and dropping a garbage bag in *Hog Wild*—we headed for downtown Stonington and a much-longed-for bacon and egg breakfast at the first greasy spoon we could find.

What is there about fried eggs served at a counter by a chubby man wearing a stained apron that tastes so much better than eggs fried at home or on a boat, for that matter? The eggs were perfect and the bacon crispy without being dry. Betsy was even satisfied with her poached egg ("*Please* don't overcook it."). Not that she's picky, it's just that if you assembled the world's top ten short-order cooks for a poach-off, nine would likely disappoint her.

The man in the stained apron, Tony, warmed to Betsy's compliments and decided to favor us with his considered political opinion. Like a great many people I had met in Maine, Tony relished his contempt for government in general and for politicians in particular. The issue of the moment was an unsigned, overdue state budget.

Tony had a solution that seemed pretty simple to me: "You have to treat them like the children they are. Remember in school, when you didn't get your work done in time? What would happen? I'll tell you: Teacher'd fail you, wouldn't she? Well, I think the politicians up in Augusta ought to be treated the same way. They don't get their work done and sign a budget in time, then they don't get paid. Simple as that."

While I was digesting that, we were joined at the counter by two small children, a little boy and a little girl, aged perhaps seven and five.

"What can I get ya?" asked Tony, his vitriol temporarily expended.

The older of the two, the boy, replied without hesitation, "One strawberry soda, a root beer, and two donuts."

Tony chuckled happily. It was 7:00 A.M. I caught his eye and knew that he too remembered the special freedom of summer vacation after a long winter in school.

Outside the Stonington Library, which had a perfect scale model of itself in its front window, I met Tim Brown. A swarthy Newfoundlander who has lived in Maine for fifteen years, Brown and his son were waiting next to the library for a ride home. While he was waiting, he told me a harrowing sea story—actually two harrowing sea stories.

The previous March, Brown had been employed as a crewman aboard the *Walter Lehman,* a 70-foot wooden dragger, when her engine room caught fire. He managed to fight his way into the smoke-filled wheel house and reached the VHF radio.

"Mayday! Mayday!" he shouted into the mike. His distress call was picked up by hundreds of fisherman, but he did not have enough time to broadcast his position. Choking, his eyes burning, he and his crewmates climbed into an emergency life raft and watched the *Walter Lehman* sink.

"God was my co-pilot that day, I can tell you," Brown said fervently. "We weren't in the raft very long. A lobsterman—he'd heard the call and spotted the smoke—picked us up an hour and a half later."

A month later Tim was out on a 38-foot gill-netter, the *T.L.C.* "You know what they say about getting right back on the horse." While they were heading in, the wash-down hose became disconnected, and the bilge filled with seawater. Before anyone realized anything was amiss the *T.L.C.* rolled over and sank. Tim and his crewmates had to swim out a porthole, and they were in the water for forty-five minutes. It must have been fearfully cold, being late April in the north Atlantic.

"Sinking twice in two months was incredible enough. I mean a guy doesn't expect to sink more than once in a lifetime. No, the really incredible thing was that the guy who pulled me out of the water—and, take it from me, we were about done for—was the same fella who was my mate on the *Walter Lehman."*

I asked him if he had been to sea since.

"As a matter of fact, no, I haven't," he said. "For the time being I'm working construction."

I was reminded of a man I'd once read about who kept getting hit by lightning. He made the *Guinness Book of World Records* as a result. No matter what he did—from *always* wearing rubber boots to getting a job working in a mine—he kept getting zapped.

"Are you nervous about going back out?" I asked Tim.

"Yeah," he replied promptly. After a moment, he added, ". . . yeah, about as nervous as a clam at low tide."

The principal part of Acadia National Park, which does not lie on Mount Desert Island or the Schoodic Peninsula is the roughly ten square miles of Isle au Haut. The more adventurous visitors to the Park take a ferry from Stonington to this quietly beautiful island, which is about as far from the bustle of Mount Desert as Machias is from Manhattan.

Our old friend Samuel de Champlain named Isle au Haut for its bold cliffs, but, if you have any doubt how Mainers pronounce it, remember this rhyme:

> Says the summer man when the fog hangs low,
> 'There's a bridal wreath o'er Isle au Haut.'
> But the fisherman says as he starts his boat,
> 'It's thick o' fog on Isle au Haut.'

"There's a bridal wreath o'er Isle au Haut."

The afternoon we pulled in between Kimball Island and the village of Isle au Haut was not foggy in the least. Instead, we took our walk in a chilly drizzle under a sky which threatened worse.

Initially we were surprised to see kitchen garden fences, which looked as secure as those of World War II stalags. Many were seven or eight feet high, and Dicken remarked that the potatoes on Isle au Haut must be awfully good. Some distance farther along we spotted a deer in the woods, then another, and then one strolled past us along the road. The deer on Isle au Haut, it turns out, are plentiful and tame, and the kind islanders (who number a mere fifty-seven in the dead of winter) are apparently content to coexist with the deer even if it means making fence-building an important island industry.

Across from the exquisitely proportioned and sturdily constructed Union Congregational Church, which has a fish-shaped weather vane, was a community center which was built by rusticators for the year-round residents. Until very recently there had been no telephone service on Isle au Haut. Now there is, as well as a public phone on the porch of the community center. Posted on a bulletin board next to it was the island telephone directory, which consisted of one typewritten, two-columned page held in place with rusty thumb tacks. There was also a sign which said: "Local calls are courtesy of the Island Telephone Company.

The ferry to Isle au Haut is island-owned and operated. It does not carry automobiles, with the happy result that there are few on the island. Those that made it there came on barges, an expensive proposition. And many of those have been on-island for a long, long time. Looking at some of the cars we passed, I got a sort of autos-of-the-living-dead feeling. Old rust buckets, whose jury-rigging has been jury-rigged and re-jury-rigged, predominate. But on the steep hill down to the ferry landing I saw a Pontiac Eight in pristine condition. The owner of this lovingly preserved gem of a motor car was taking no chances whatsoever. Chocked behind the left rear wheel was a wooden lobster buoy to prevent the car from rolling backwards into the sea.

Union Congregational Church, Isle au Haut.

We made it back to *Consolation* just as the skies made good on their threat. The downpour was brief, however, and we were able to get under way for the twelve-mile hop across Isle au Haut Bay to Vinalhaven. Unfortunately, the hop turned into more of a crawl as the wind and rain died together. For one of the very few times during the summer, we had to trade our mainsail for the Iron Main. We motored across the bay and, eventually, around the southern end of Vinalhaven.

If you think of Penobscot Bay as a large container, then Vinalhaven Island is its plug—centered smack in the middle—forcing unimaginable quantities of water to one side or the other as the tides fill the bay. Off Vinalhaven, a little to the southwest, is a small island with an extraordinary history and a thought-provoking name: Hurricane.

As luck would have it, I recognized the first person I met as we landed at the dock of the Hurricane Island Outward Bound School. It had been twelve years since I had seen Judy Lawson, a wiry, deeply tanned woman with long white-blonde hair with whom I had once collaborated on a magazine piece.

For the past eleven years Judy, who once completed a *solo* trans-Atlantic crossing, had been a sailing instructor at the Hurricane Island Outward Bound School (HIOBS). We could not have had a better guide.

Judy led Betsy, Eliza, and me away from the center of the HIOBS encampment on the east side of Hurricane, past the fresh water quarry where a group was learning rappelling, to the awe-inspiring ropes course. The Outward Bound philosophy, Judy explained, is to challenge, inspire, and motivate. Whether flying down a zip line on the ropes course, hanging off the side of a cliff, or enduring a storm in one of the sprit-rigged Hurricane Island pulling boats, the idea is to transform such

Seal Bay, Vinalhaven.

challenges into heightened self-confidence and self-esteem.

Nowhere was this more evident than on the ropes course. The day we happened to visit was an "invitational," which meant that a group of grown men and women had been invited to the island for a day to get a taste of the Outward Bound experience in the hope that they would volunteer some future financial support.

When Outward Bound began, it was aimed at young people. Betsy, for example, went to Outward Bound at age twenty in the Three Sisters Wilderness Area of Oregon and loved every minute of it. Dicken, at seventeen, went to the one in the Cascades in Washington State. Now people of all ages attend some thirty different Outward Bound Schools worldwide.

A man named Victor was being urged to complete a particularly hair-raising leg of the ropes course while we watched. Beneath his blue mountaineering helmet, he looked petrified. Sweat poured down a face that was already an alarming shade of purple. He was hesitating at the jumping-off platform of the zip line and seemed unable to give himself the final push. He looked like he would have been a lot happier not to have to zoom out of control down a fifty-foot high zip line into a rope net. His partner cajoled him with encouragements like "You can do it, Vic!" "Go for it!"

It was touch and go for several tense minutes. Suddenly, Victor let out a primal scream and, with a face that shrieked *I'm-gonna-die,* he let go.

Watching Victor's expression turn into one of intense pride after his success-

Victor on the Outward Bound ropes course.

Two sprit sail, ketch-rigged Hurricane Island Outward Bound School pulling boats off Pemaquid Point.

ful landing made it easier to understand the Outward Bound experience. He was so incredibly pleased with himself, surrounded as he was by his partner and the rest of his group. They all hugged him and clapped him on the back. He had the look of a man quite different than the one who, moments earlier, had released himself into the unknown.

On the way back to *Hoggie* we passed a derelict steam-driven air compressor with an enormous rusted flywheel more than six feet in diameter. "That," said Judy, pointing, "is the other part of the Hurricane Island story, the chapter that ended in 1915."

The period following the Civil War had been an era of great prosperity for the North. The Union had experienced a surge of patriotic fervor. What better way to satisfy both conditions than to build monuments to the heroic fallen and monumental buildings for the thriving survivors and their heirs? And what better building material than granite? The builders looked to the granitic domes of Maine islands like Vinalhaven, Crotch, Mt. Desert, Swans, Deer Isle, and Hurricane to feed this flurry of construction and to the immense fleet of Maine coastal schooners for inexpensive delivery.

Hurricane Island was by no means the greatest producer of granite during this golden age, but it had one of the most compelling and poignant histories.

In 1870 William Vinal, the son of the man for whom Vinalhaven was named, sold a small, nearby island called Hurricane to a one-footed Civil War veteran named Davis Tillson. Like the purchase of Manhattan from the Indians or Alaska from the Russians (Seward's Folly), Tillson paid Vinal a ridiculous low price for the island: Fifty dollars. Then again, Vinal didn't think it was worth much more.

To Tillson, an aggressive, obsessive former Yankee general, it was a gold mine, or, rather, a granite mine. In no time at all there was a thriving community on Hurricane—850 people from Maine, Sweden, Norway, Finland, Scotland, Wales, Ireland, and, especially from Italy, expert stonecutters, polishers, and carvers. The Scots took to calling their energetic new boss "Lord of the Isles." The Italians had a nickname for Tillson which probably better reflected his personality; they called him *"Bombasto Furioso."*

With Tillson firmly in control of the Hurricane Granite Company, both business and the growing island community flourished. Soon Hurricane had its own post office, a company store, a school, and a church. By 1880 it had three dozen cottages, two principal quarries, a bandstand, and a bowling green. There were bachelor-only boardinghouses and Anarchy Hall where the granite men met to argue about socialism, play cards and checkers, and, no doubt, gripe about General Tillson's iron hand.

They were not griping all the time though; their output was prodigious. One clever foreman is even credited with inventing the ball bearing on Hurricane. The granite loaders used massive cranes to lift the blocks of granite, but they had no system for rotating the loads out over the wharves where they could be lowered into the holds of coastal schooners. This one fellow grooved the plate at the base of the derrick in a circle, did the same to a mating plate, and in between them set half a dozen Civil War–surplus cannon balls. When they were all greased up, the derrick rotated as smoothly as your grandma's lazy Susan.

Before the end came so abruptly to this proud period, Hurricane's granite men had shipped finished stonework to a pretty impressive list of clients. They included the Brooklyn Bridge, the Library of Congress, the United States Naval Academy, Boston's Suffolk County Courthouse, the Washington Monument, the municipalities of New York and Boston (paving stones for the streets), and, curiously, Havana, Cuba (an order of thirty-three thousand cobblestones). One of my favorite buildings in New York, the glorious Beaux Arts New York Custom House on Bowling Green, was built in large part with Hurricane Island granite. Indeed, few Americans have not had occasion to admire the product of this unusual place sometime, somewhere, in some public building or some monument.

At the beginning of the twentieth century the rosy-hued granite of Maine lost the competition among building materials, first to concrete, then to artificial stone, and finally to steel and glass. In 1915 the end to life on Hurricane came with the abruptness of a slamming door. One day the island bustled with activity. In its heyday there were twelve hundred workers and their families perched on an island less than three-quarters of a mile long. The next, the company store closed and panicky families rushed to make the last scheduled boat back to Carvers Harbor. Many left behind on Hurricane everything they owned; some returned later for abandoned possessions, and a few of the island houses were actually moved elsewhere. We saw at least one in Castine.

Overnight, Hurricane Island became a ghost town not to be reinhabited for fifty years until the Hurricane Island Outward Bound School was established in 1964.

Judy Lawson led us back toward the dock. We passed carved stone blocks, finished pieces that remained precisely where they had been the day of the final exodus from Hurricane.

I have a colonial house in Connecticut, the oldest part of which is two hundred years old. Just as I sometimes do there, I closed my eyes on Hurricane and tried to bring alive the ghosts who had lived there—the ghosts of the granite men, the Scottish quarrymen, the Italian stonecutters, the Irish paving cutters, and the granite polishers from Maine. I tried to imagine the teams of oxen straining under the weight of a hundred tons of granite pulling colossal galamanders with wheels taller than a man. I could nearly hear the ping of sledgehammer on plug wedge splitting granite blocks apart, the roar of steam engines powering the stone drills,

One of the quarries at Hurricane: Climbing has replaced carving.

and the thump of dynamite blasting great hunks free. When I opened my eyes, all I could hear in the distance was a shout of encouragement from one Outward Bounder to another and then the splash of someone taking a cooling dip in the abandoned quarry.

The strangest thing is that after all these years the Maine granite business is having a tiny resurgence. The recent restoration of the Statute of Liberty used Maine granite. Not long ago New England Stone Industries, a Rhode Island concern, reopened an operation on Crotch Island, and Crotch's Goss Quarry is once again supplying the grander construction projects of Boston and New York.

The Crotch Island operation has reopened. Pink granite from Crotch was the stone Jacqueline Kennedy chose for her slain husband's gravesite at Arlington National Cemetery.

Like Zen monks watching carrots grow, Betsy and I sat on a round rock staring at The Basin and waited for the tide to turn. The Basin is an inlet halfway up the west coast of Vinalhaven with a reversing fall similar to but smaller than the one down east at Cobscook.

As we sat there, I was reminded of a jolly prayer I had seen quoted in Duncan and Ware's cruising guide:

Lord, we thank thee that thy Grace
    Has brought us to this pleasant place.
And most earnestly we pray
    That other folk will stay away.

Happily the "other folk" did. That morning we had The Basin entirely to ourselves and were selfishly grateful for the privilege. I had never been there before, but Betsy had many times. In fact, visiting The Basin was one of her treasured childhood memories: sitting on that same rock with her father, waiting for slack tide when you can row inside. As on Hurricane where ghosts abound, there was one at The Basin for Betsy.

Betsy has sailed the Maine coast all her life—many more times than I have—with her father, Gib Kittredge, and his boyhood friend, Fred Crane. After the nineteenth summer of Betsy's life, her father died of cancer at the age of forty-five. One day he was fine, as alive as a man can be, navigating *Caution* through the Halifax Race; the next, he died the sort of sudden death that makes you scream, *Unfair!* He left a shattered family: a young widow, four kids.

Fred and Joyce Crane took up some of the slack. Acting as surrogate parents,

The reversing falls at The Basin, Vinalhaven.

they continued the summer cruises in Maine, always including Betsy and Kathy, Peter and Coe as they did their own children.

As with love songs, associating a special place with a special person—particularly a departed loved one—is a common enough phenomenon. Although she did not actually say it, I imagined some old memories were floating through her mind as we sat there in companionable silence.

Finally the water at the narrow mouth of The Basin was still. I rowed *Hoggie* through the cut. Betsy sat astern drinking in the incredible beauty of the place. The silence was interrupted only by the dipping of my oars and the splash of ospreys diving for fish. Occasionally, a fish would break the placid waters, probably dodging harbor seals. Every once in a while a brown sausage of a seal would appear, stare curiously at us, and then slip noiselessly back below the glassy surface.

It was a sublime three-quarters of an hour for a married couple to spend together.

Thirteen

PERMISSIVE TRESPASS

INSOFAR AS the often flimsy social fabric of island life is concerned, nowhere does it seem more finely woven than on North Haven. Summer folk and year-rounders seem to coexist here better than most other places we had been. I am sure there are countless feuds and local squabbles a visitor wouldn't be able to uncover for years, but on the surface at least the people of North Haven just seem to get along.

This is no ordinary collection of rusticators, I might add. Old money abounds, and newcomers are in short supply. The money is quiet, the houses, unpretentious, but the names bellow influence, wealth, and power. Among the privileged summer folk are Cabots, Lamonts, Morgans, Rockefellers, and the Watsons of IBM. In the old days Charles Lindbergh used to fly into a private airstrip to visit his in-laws, the Morrows, who still summer on the island.

Intermarriage between the islanders and the summer people has been a factor in strengthening the peaceful coexistence between the two groups. It has also helped a younger generation of islanders to afford to stay on island. The North Haven Foundation collects money from year-rounders and summer folk alike to provide scholarships so that any resident of the island will be able to attend college; the fund also provides for housing subsidies so that the island housing market is not completely dominated by the upward pressure of vacation home buyers from Boston and New York. North Haven may be the only place in America where the trickle-down theory of economics has any meaning.

In the village of North Haven our guide, Jamie Carpenter, a friend from New York and a fifteen-year summer resident, was explaining the island's convoluted social structure to me when he interrupted himself to point to a pristine Model T Ford putt-putting past Foy Brown's boatyard. At the wheel was an elderly gent wearing a blue seersucker jacket and a white straw hat who gave us a cheery wave as he drove past. "That, for example, is Tom Watson," said Jamie. I would soon discover that receiving a friendly wave—like getting picked up hitchhiking—was something we could expect more of in this contented place.

Acknowledging strangers is serious business in Maine. It is an exercise undertaken neither lightly nor thoughtlessly, and the means and style are all-important.

Friendly summer types tend to give an open-handed wave. But the native Mainer, I have observed, generally uses a more economical gesture. You might even call it minimalist. A forefinger touched to the brim of a cap in a discrete salute might be all that you would see. Smiles and a heartier wave are optional. None of this, however, diminishes the worth of the salutation.

For instance, later that day we saw an old-timer in a red pick-up truck driving toward us at a leisurely pace. Eliza and I were walking along the dusty shoulder of Crabtree Point Road toward Pulpit Harbor. When he came abreast, I caught his eye. He had both hands gripping the top of the wheel. In an elegantly subtle acknowledgment—one which could have been overlooked by an inattentive visitor—he lifted just the forefingers of each hand and made a motion like two miniature windshield wipers going in opposite directions. That was it; then he was gone. I felt as if he'd kissed us.

Foy Brown's boatyard, North Haven.

Coastal cruising inevitably turns even the most well-mannered crew into accomplished freeloaders. We were no exception. After almost no hinting whatsoever, the Carpenters took us in and spoiled us rotten with extravagant meals and splendid company. I had forgotten what it was like to lie down on soft white sheets, which—mirable dictu!—were dry.

Jamie Carpenter, his wife, Toshiko Mori, and their daughter, Tei, live in a charming 1796 farmhouse built on a hill overlooking Cubby Hole Cove. When Cubby Hole Farm was still working, its grassy hillside was thick with grazing cows and the milk was taken out by boat at high tide. At low tide the Cubby Hole ebbs nearly to dry.

Jamie is a sculptor whose medium is glass; Toshiko, an architect with a thriving practice, among whose recent commissions was the restructuring of the Farnsworth Library and Art Museum in Rockland.

They took us to visit their artist friend, Eric Hopkins. Like the bold, wild colors of his Maine landscapes, Eric is kinetic, frenetic, sometimes frantic, but always, always a character. If you ask him a question like, "How old are your kids?" quick as a flash, he would answer, "Two and three-quarters and three-quarters." It's not that he's a wise-ass; it's just the way his mind works. He paints to the blare of rock music, his radio hot-wired to an automobile battery. There is no power in his out-of-the-way studio except that supplied by the battery and his own overcharged personality.

We watched him transmute a scribbled pencil sketch into a finished painting while maintaining a monologue about his art and technique—loud enough to be heard over the music. While he worked, he jabbed at his paintings, executed sweeping brush strokes, and gesticulated wildly with his free hand. His brush moved like the baton of a conductor trying to direct the Led Zeppelin song he was listening to rather than a Beethoven sonata.

Hopkins makes Pee Wee Herman seem catatonic.

"I get a real fast, instant response from the landscape I grew up with. You could say I'm a responsivist," he shouted as he mixed a hot shade of pink. "I guess one day that will make me a neo-responsivist," he laughed in a way that said *I don't hold much truck with the traditional art world.*

Like the bold, wild colors of his Maine landscapes, Eric Hopkins is kinetic, frenetic, sometimes frantic, but always, always a character.

He gestured out the window to a field of wildflowers and sun-dappled Southern Harbor beyond. "I just respond to what I see and feel out there. I soak it up then I respond again in the studio. Sometimes I feel like I'm confronting the environment while it's confronting me."

Suddenly, he dropped his brush on a table piled high with paint tubes and thick with coffee cans full of brushes. He took his wet painting by the top two corners and danced over to the wall where he attached it with push pins. Dancing back to the beat of the "Material Girl," he seized a blank sheet, laid it on a clean piece of Masonite, and grabbed a fresh brush.

"This one's gonna be a gooser!" he announced. "Lots of bursting out energy stuff!"

I had no doubt it would. I didn't like his work at first, but by the time I left I felt altogether different about it. Perhaps his personal energy influenced me, but as we said good-bye I looked again at the wall full of drying paintings and each one was so full of that energy, so full of drop-dead punch, I departed a major fan.

Eric is not the only spark plug in his family. He has a brother Will who went to Harvard and is a Cambridge computer whiz. His brother David works at the Metropolitan Museum of Art in New York; his father was a published author. But his mother, June, just might be the most interesting of all.

June Hopkins had thought right from the start that there was something a little strange about Martin Godgart, the new teacher of French, Latin, and English at the North Haven High School. It was 1957, and she would have ample opportunity to get to know him, because Godgart and her husband had become fine friends and drinking buddies. The new teacher would often stop by to tip the elbow with Bill Hopkins at their home.

In spite of the fact that Godgart was hugely popular with the students (he was troop leader of the Sea Scouts, led the Baptist Sunday school, and posed as Santa Claus for the children of North Haven), June continued to have a nagging doubt about Martin Godgart, although she couldn't put her finger on exactly why. There was something mysterious, even evil, she often thought. After one cocktail visit, she surreptitiously wrapped his whiskey glass in a handkerchief and sent it to the FBI. Bingo! The fingerprints of the man who called himself Martin Godgart and one Ferdinand Waldo Demara, Jr., were the same.

For more than eighteen years Ferdinand Waldo Demara, Jr., a chubby confidence man who never finished high school, had pursued a fantastic avocation: He had assumed the identities and careers of countless professionals all over the United States and Canada.

Among these coloful episodes had been a stint as a Canadian naval surgeon, during which he performed scores of delicate operations, including the resection of a lung and the removal of a bullet a mere fraction of an inch from a South Korean soldier's heart. He had been an auditor at a Texas hotel, a cancer re-

From the end of Rockland's mile-long breakwater, a man waves his hat in greeting as the windjamming passenger schooner *Heritage* returns to her home port.

Bear Island, Penobscot Bay.

searcher, a teacher of psychology and a psychiatrist ("There's no mystery about psychiatry," he had once said. "Anybody with common sense could practice it."), a Catholic monk in ten states and in Canada (he twice converted to Catholicism although he was born Roman Catholic), a college dean in Pennsylvania, and a deputy sheriff in Thurston County, Washington.

In Ferdinand Waldo Demara, Jr., June Hopkins had unmasked The Great Impostor, the man *Life* Magazine later called "a genius, the greatest impostor of our time."

Because of June's detective work, Demara was arrested and convicted of misrepresentation. But in the end he only received a suspended sentence because the jury concluded he had done no lasting harm. (The jury also thought that he had done a fine job teaching their children.)

We said our good-byes to Jamie and Toshiko, hosts and tour-guides extraordinaire. Leaving the village of North Haven behind we sailed around to the top of the island. There, in one of the prettiest harbors in Penobscot Bay, we dropped the hook for the night.

Dominated by a cluster of houses owned by the Cabots, Cabot Cove lies to the west of the entrance to Pulpit Harbor. Often one or two of the big windjamming schooners like the *Isaac H. Evans, Roseway,* or *Heritage* spend the night in Pulpit. Sometimes, if the wind is right, I am told, they even come in under sail,

Cabot Cove, Pulpit Harbor, North Haven Island.

which must be a majestic sight. We nestled in Cabot Cove between a North Haven dingy and a Herreshoff 12½.

Besides being one of the most graceful small sailing sloops afloat, the 12½ was for many years the most popular. The first 12½ was built in 1914; it is astonishing to note that the first dozen 12½'s ever built are still fully operational and moored in and around North Haven, Maine. The gaff-rigged North Haven Dinghy, which, like the Herreshoff, is another beauty of a wooden sloop, is a member of the oldest single one-design class of racing sailboats in the world. North Haveners started racing them in 1887. As we watched the sun set over the Camden Hills, we felt good resting in such distinguished company.

The next morning, a Sunday, was as tranquil as a day can be. The surface of Pulpit Harbor was mill-pond flat. Objects above the shoreline reflected perfectly in the water below. You could take a photograph that morning, turn it upside down, and never know the difference.

I rose just after sunup, careful not to disturb Betsy, Eliza, and Dicken; it was a heavenly morning for a solitary row. As I rounded the point which hides harbor from cove, I could see in the distance another boat, a twin scull, slicing effortlessly through the still waters. With no perceptible breath of air it was easy to hear the conversation of the couple who were rowing out toward Pulpit Rock. I felt vaguely guilty eavesdropping . . . they were so obviously in the throes of budding summer love.

HE: You're such a good rower.
SHE: Oh, I am not. You're the one who's so good at it.
HE: No, I'm not just saying that. You row so beautifully.
SHE: Really? Do I?

Just as Martin Luther King's name became synonymous with the civil rights movement, Betty Friedan's with the women's movement, and Ralph Nader with consumer advocacy, there would be no Island Institute without a determined leader named Philip W. Conkling. Operating out of a small office on the waterfront in Rockland, he heads an organization dedicated to the well-being and survival—in both natural and human respects—of the three thousand plus Maine islands. The Institute's motto is succinct: Sustaining Islands and Their Communities.

Part of the Institute's mission is to communicate—a job it excels at. The *Island News* is a widely read twenty-four-page quarterly newsletter mailed free to every Maine island boxholder. The annual *Island Journal* is a glossy magazine as visually sophisticated as *Vermont Life* or *Arizona Highways.*

Central to the Island Institute philosophy is the "balanced use" of Maine's islands, and balancing the needs of both year-round and seasonal communities would be a daunting task for any Executive Director. Philip Conkling just seems particularly well-equipped to tackle it. Naturalist, forester, administrator, lecturer, fund-raiser, publisher, and author, Conkling patrols his beloved islands on a powerful launch with Island Institute painted in bold, black letters down both sides. He is a knowledgeable, articulate advocate, unafraid of a fight, and he has become a force to be reckoned with along the coast. Don't miss Conkling's book, *Islands in Time: A Natural and Human History of the Islands of Maine,* if you have *any* interest in any aspect of "islandness."

Just as we did with the Carpenters, I called Conkling out of the blue the same day I wanted to visit him. He did not know me from Adam but, after hearing that I was researching a book, said, "Okay, come around after lunch."

"Requests like mine must be a dime-a-dozen," I said, smiling, as I took the proffered seat. I was in my icebreaking mode.

The windows in his office overlooked a rather homely corner of Rockland's working harbor. Outside a steady rain beat against the glass.

"Regrettably, yes," he said dryly. He was dressed like a bruise, black sweater and blue jeans.

I tried again. "Well, what made you decide to see me then?"

"It's just a question of too much to do in too little time. Most people who call like you did are *planning* to write a book about Maine. I can't be in the position of helping people prepare book proposals. I'm meeting you because you *are* writing a book about Maine."

No nonsense about this guy, I thought. But in spite of a rocky start he gave generously of his time and knowledge. I asked him scads of questions, which he patiently answered. The bias of his counsel struck me as a valuable one.

I was especially interested in his perspective on the impact of the ever growing numbers of visiting pleasure boats to the coast. I had noted some interesting discrepancies in the two cruising guides we used aboard *Consolation,* the publishing dates of which are separated by twenty years. Under the entry for Trafton Island in Narraguagus Bay, for example, Duncan and Ware (1968 edition) stated: "This is one of the most attractive islands on the coast. . . . The woods are grown up enough so that walking is not difficult. . . . At high water on a warm day the swimming on the beach in the northern cove is good and there may still be some clams on the flats. . . ."

By contrast, twenty years later, the Tafts wrote: "Trafton has been privately owned by one family for decades, and the owners are in residence much of the summer. Because so many people have come ashore uninvited in recent years, the owners now request that you *not* land unless invited." Quite a difference. Even some friends of mine, who have owned an island in the middle of Penobscot Bay for three generations, have resorted to No Trespassing signs for the first time ever, and it nearly killed them to do so.

Guiding light of the Island Institute, Philip Conkling, at the Camden Yacht Club.

I remember Fred Crane's blunt thoughts on the subject when I was in the planning stage of this trip: "One of the nice things about cruising in Maine has always been that you could land on any island and you would care for the island as if it were your own. Now the jackasses have ruined this for everyone."

"What," I asked Conkling, "is the problem? Fires? Litter? Vandalism?"

"No, it's simpler. It's just too many boats. Almost by definition the idea of solitude is wrapped up in the idea of islands. So what we're dealing with here is not an environmental carrying-capacity issue; it is a *psychological* carrying-capacity issue. There was a time when the informal rule was 'permissive trespass' and it was okay to land your dinghy on someone's beach because there weren't very many of you. That era has unfortunately passed."

One good reason for the "magic of Maine" (i.e., significantly fewer yachts than in places like Long Island Sound or Chesapeake Bay) had always been fear. Many sailors were simply too scared to venture up a coast with as many hazards as Maine's: hidden ledges, rocky shores, horrific tides, and, of course, the dreaded dungeon thick o' fog.

"Why," I asked Conkling, "has that changed? Why so many more boats?"

"In a word: technology. Now, there's Loran-C, SatNav, and GPS." (All three are electronic aids to navigation, but G[lobal] P[ositioning] S[ystem] is the newest and most precise. Triangulating with satellites, GPS in its military version has astonishing accuracy: precision locating down to one *centimeter* is routine.) Conkling continued, "It used to be that if you had money it still did not mean you could navigate along the Maine coast. You still needed real skills. Now you can write a check for that ability, and it doesn't even cost that much."

Samuel Eliot Morison, Christopher Columbus's biographer and Mount Desert Island's historian, was on to this notion years earlier when he wrote, "Nowadays, any fool with a radar and a fathometer-equipped boat can roar through the thoroughfares as easily as he can drive a car."

After talking to Conkling, I felt more a part of the problem than a part of the solution. Although we were more seat-of-the-pants sailors than electronics experts

(*Consolation* is not equipped with GPS, and I am apparently too stupid to fine-tune the Loran sufficiently to trust it in a real pea-souper), we were—fair's fair—one more sailboat crowding Maine's waters.

We didn't litter. We tried not to trespass. We never lit a fire above the high waterline, or anywhere ashore, for that matter. But we were undeniably part of the crowd.

To atone, let me pass along three simple thoughts that have occurred to me while I have enjoyed the islands of this diminishing frontier. These thoughts are obvious, perhaps, to many, but too easily forgotten by a few. Together they form an elementary code of conduct for low-impact enjoyment of a wilderness area. And they apply to each and every one of us whether we see this magnificent coast out the window of a car driving up Route 1 or are fortunate enough to visit it by sea.

- Whatever else you do, have respect for the environment.
- Respect the wishes of landowners and their desire for solitude. Do this, and Day-Glo No Trespassing signs will not be the only things that your descendants see when they visit Maine.
- Finally, if you will forgive a venerable cliché, *do* take only photographs and leave nothing but your footprints.

On a small, privately owned island in the Deer Island Thorofare there is an especially enlightened and eloquent plea to those who land there. It takes the form of a discreet sign printed with these words:

> In their absence, the owners know that
> they are dependent on your good judgment
> and sense of fitness as to what you do.
> If you value privacy and beauty, surely
> you will understand that the owners
> treasure the land on which you stand.

Aerial view of Camden harbor. Tiny Curtis Island Light beckons approaching mariners.

Fourteen
THE OUTER ISLANDS

WILD STRAWBERRIES, blueberries, blackberries, cranberries, and raspberries dot the seven hundred acres of Matinicus, the outermost of the inhabited Maine islands. Thirty-six different varieties of ferns and seventeen varieties of orchids thrive here. In the summer wild apple trees provide shade for meadows filled with lupine, buttercups, and wild roses.

And wild is a good word to describe the rest of this remote and beautiful place. Matinicus is what is left of the tip of the end of one of the mountain ranges carved eons ago by the glaciers. Fifty-six hardy souls comprise the present population, and—an abundance of summer flowers and fruit notwithstanding—life is tough. If the island of Frenchboro struck you as a difficult place to spend a winter, Matinicus would, I suspect, be too forbidding even to consider.

The ferry comes once a month; the school's enrollment is down to four children; there is no hotel, movie theater, bowling alley, or supermarket; and the general store—called the Off Shore Store—now closes during the winter for lack of off-season patrons. Politically, Matinicus is still incorporated as a Plantation rather than a town; a trio of Town Fathers are in charge. Electricity and telephone service only arrived in the 1960s. Today the island-owned power company has the distinction of being the smallest self-generating public utility in the world.

One lifelong islander, Donna Rogers, put it this way: "Matinicus is not just a place but a 'way of life.' " She described the sort of qualities an islander must possess to hack it there: "Quiet fortitude, strong wills, and independence must be part of their life-style. They must have uncommon patience and acceptance of things that can't be changed, but the island also offers to those who live here a life not quite like anywhere else."

I introduced myself at the door of her log house, which is perched atop Harbor Point with a view of the comings and goings of Matinicus Harbor. There was nothing cool about her greeting—quite the contrary, her eyes crinkled into a smile—but she said she could only talk to me if I did not mind her continuing to work.

"Not all women do as much as I do," she said with a self-deprecating shrug. "I'm afraid I'm a workaholic." Workaholic doesn't *begin* to describe this Pioneer Woman, an indisputable Jill-of-all-trades. Even though her husband lobsters year-round (their son is his sternman), Donna, as she puts it, "stays busy." Staying busy means she has written and published a history of Matinicus; she caretakes two houses owned by summer people; last winter she fed a work crew who were renovating a summer house, and she later joint-compounded ("It took twenty-five gallons to get those walls smooth again!") and painted the upstairs of the same house; she's also the other kind of painter and sells her landscapes to island visitors; and in her spare times she runs a restaurant. Rogers serves lobster dinners on her back porch. Her table d'hôte costs $10.95, "includin' all the fixin's." I could smell an oven full of potatoes baking while we talked.

Oh, and she raised three children and has two grandchildren.

Her budding restaurant business is suddenly in jeopardy, however. In a bizarre twist on conventional real estate practices, another family built a rival restaurant right smack between Donna Rogers's log house and the harbor. Anywhere else this would be patently illegal. Only in twentieth-century Maine (and possibly the Wild West before the Louisiana Purchase) could such a thing happen. The other restaurant is a big barn-like affair, which blocks not all but some of Rogers's fine harbor view. It clings to the side of Harbor Point the way houses are grafted onto the cliffsides of the Hollywood Hills or the mudslides of Malibu—with a combination of cantilevers, pilings, and, one imagines, prayers. It is also close enough so that a diner at Donna's could reach over to the other restaurant for a jar of Grey Poupon.

"How could this have happened?" I asked.

"We had this area up here for twenty-five years all to ourselves. Perfect spot, perfect view. But, you see, here in Maine they have something called 'undivided land.' That means that a number of people can inherit shares in a plot of land, but nobody has ever specified *which* shares.

Old-style bentwood lobster pots are piled on a Matinicus pier.

"Harbor Point is 'undivided land,' and the rule is that you can build anywhere you want as long as it's more than "one ox-cart width" from the next guy's house."

I was frankly incredulous. I remember hearing about anachronistic blue laws while I was in college. For instance, an unaccompanied woman could not legally stand at a bar in Connecticut at that time, or, when traveling by vehicle at night in Massachusetts, a companion was required to walk ahead holding a lit lantern. But such laws were, for practical purposes, unenforceable. Not so in Maine where common, undivided ownership of land remains an active legal principle, the likes of which can ruin nascent businesses like Donna Rogers's restaurant.

Donna Rogers.

Was she worried, I asked. But before she answered, I knew that a woman as enterprising and resilient as Donna Rogers would never bow to such a discouragement. I wondered at the same time if life on Matinicus would be viable without as many skills and resources as she seemed to possess.

"I believe in the free enterprise system," she explained simply. "I believe if I do a good job, I'll be all right. If I serve a good meal, if people don't leave hungry, if they go away happy and satisfied; well, I can stand up to any competition likely to come my way. And if I can't, I'll move on to something else.

"I'll be fine. It's the island I'm worried about. We're hurting for people, for sheer numbers. Winters get pretty iffy because we're down to twenty to twenty-five people. We have four children in school this year. Now we've been down to two when my kids were little. People think that this is bad, but we've seen worse than this. Still, it's hard to see a rosy glow in the distance. . . ."

In case my characterization has given you the impression of a humorless individual, don't entertain that thought one minute longer. This is an excerpt from her self-published booklet, *Tales of Matinicus Island: History, Lore, and Legend:*

Matinicus Terminology

Native—One whose ancestors are buried here and whose family goes back at least a hundred years. There are no exceptions to the rule, but once in a while if you've lived here more than twenty years, you may be called one by mistake.

Islander—One who lives here and goes lobstering. He must put in at least one winter with the natives or at least prove himself useful to the Island.

Summer Person—One who owns a home here and visits periodically, usually in the summer. He pays taxes, supports the Island, attends Town Meetings, but has no vote or say in local government. His status never changes, no matter how long he comes here, unless he claims residency, and then only under duress.

Damned Summer Person—One who does something that the Islanders don't like or doesn't stay out of local politics.

Sternman—That steadfast young man who stands in the stern of the boat all day and eats saltwater and bait.

Sternperson—A girl stern-man.

Yahoo—One of those young idiots who live in the top of trap shops and irritate the neighbors with his drinking, loud motorcycles and fast cars—or everybody's sternman but yours.

There was much to be gained from shooting the breeze with Donna Rogers. It became obvious, though, that I had taken more than my share of her time. Not that she said anything; there was no suggestion of impoliteness. I could just feel it. Time to leave her to the rest of her dinner preparations—or to whatever else she might devise to eke out a living on this lonely outpost.

I left marveling at her optimism and self-reliance. "You have to be very self-motivated, very self-contained, very patient," she had said.

When I got back to *Consolation,* Eliza had befriended two girls, and they were aboard visiting. The threesome—Samantha, (eight); Crystal, (eight); and Eliza, (nine)—were nearly perfectly matched in age.

Eliza proudly showed them *Consolation*'s saloon, the bunk she slept on, where she stowed her watercolors and markers, and other important features of her home-away-from-home. Samantha and Crystal politely made it clear that they had been aboard "tons of yachts" and were steadfastly nonchalant as they peered into every nook and cranny below decks.

Crystal and Samantha came back into the cockpit, each with a handful of M&M's and each with a smile. Whatever envy they may have felt for Eliza's "yacht" had quickly melted in their mouths. So much for the insecurities of island children. Betsy offered them some juice and went below to get it.

I took the opportunity to ask them about school. Samantha said that the only other students were her brother Nick, (ten), and "Crystal's boyfriend . . . well, maybe not her boyfriend, but she *does* have a crush on him."

"Do not." Crystal had turned the color of a freshly boiled lobster, and she glared maliciously at Samantha.

While we were talking, I had been watching a boy circling *Consolation* in an outboard. He was studiously ignoring us.

"Who's that?" I asked.

Samantha said, "Oh that's Nick. He's my brother. He's a jerk."

I was relieved to see that the children of Matinicus were no different than any other red-blooded American kid.

Eliza piped in, "Want to go for a ride in *Hoggie?*"

"Sure."

"Yeah, let's go over to Wheaton Island."

I watched them wriggle into their lifejackets, listened to them complain about having to do so, and helped them climb into *Hoggie.* Dicken had been coaching Eliza all summer in the subtleties of rowing, and it was with a certain pride that she took the oars. I think she may have realized she was being scrutinized by two experts. She rowed strongly and steadily. Her wake showed none of the serpentine shape of the novice oarsman. The tips of her oars sliced splashlessly into the water.

I could hear them chattering happily as *Hoggie* quickly drew away. Betsy and I looked at one another, and I think we were both thinking the same thing. A nine-year-old can learn a lot spending a summer at sea.

Through Donna Rogers I met seventy-five-year-old Clayton Young, former proprietor of Young's Store, former postmaster, unofficial island historian, and a

Dicken had been coaching Eliza all summer in the subtleties of rowing, and it was with a certain pride that she took the oars.

slightly tubby, slightly naughty lifelong Matinician. I went to visit him while Betsy, Eliza, and Dicken went to explore the beach on the southern end of the island.

He led me into his snug house away from the noise of two men installing a new septic system. The house was on the main north-south road north of the crossroads. The gray shingles had clearly weathered many a winter gale, but inside it was airy and cheerful.

"Welcome to Matinicus, heart of the good lobster country!" he said right off. "I've heard people say that they won't eat lobster anywhere else on the coast of Maine 'cept here. The lobster here tastes so much better, is why.

"I suppose you want to ask me how come an old man like me would live in such a godforsaken place. That it? Well, I'll tell you. One reason is that I hate city life. I like to be able to spread my arms and not hit somebody in the face. You can sure get that here. 'Course it *is* pretty lonely and boring."

A large cat rubbed against my legs, purring loudly.

"What's his name?" I asked.

"Her." Young corrected me. "I hesitate to tell you, but her name is Happy. My son named her. Whenever I want her to come inside, I have to skulk around the yard calling out 'Happy! Happy!' It makes me feel like a damn fool."

We talked for a few minutes about politics and relations between the islanders and the ever-burgeoning summer population.

Clayton Young. " 'Guess you can see,' he concluded with evident pride, 'why I'm known as the town grump.' "

"I know it's hard," he said, "and I know they mean well. But you can see how we might not like to have people come out here and *immediately* want to change us. You're not doing this right; you're not doing that right. Well, the same thing's been done for a hundred years and it's served us well enough. No doubt its old potatoes to them, but it works for us.

"We've had 'em come out here and try to take the church over. God knows it probably needs it, but it is our church. When it comes to island politics (to tell you the truth, there isn't that much going on as far as island politics is concerned), but what there is of it is ours. And why shouldn't we keep it that way?"

It seemed like a reasonable request.

Young's family was among the earliest settlers on Matinicus. I asked him to tell me about his family. He suggested we take a tour in his pick-up truck while we talked. "Before we go, I'd better make sure there's enough fuel." He ducked into the barn and returned with a jerry can, which he used to pour gasoline into the truck. "Don't have a fillin' station here yet," he said over his shoulder.

I piled in next to him, narrowly missing an exposed seat spring. He chuckled. Affectionately patting the dash, he said, "She doesn't have many miles on her—the island's only two miles long after all—but this truck's older 'n God and every bit as dependable." He let out the clutch and the maroon pick-up lurched into reverse.

"The history of Matinicus," Clayton Young began, "is the same as the history of just a few families: mostly the Halls, the Ameses, and the Youngs.

"My family was one of the first families on the island, but not *the* first. The Halls have that distinction. Ebenezer Hall and his wife were the first settlers. They were the only white people here. Once in a while they were visited by Penobscot Indians gathering birds and eggs and fish. But mostly they were alone.

"After a couple of years, Ebenezer took his wife Suzannah home to visit her folks who lived down Kittery-way. When they returned, she threw an ultimatum at him: I'm not coming back unless another family comes with us. And that second family that came here was mine, headed by old Abraham Young."

At the end of the north-south road lies a beautiful crescent-shaped strip of white sand called South Sandy Beach. It was the first rockless beach we had seen since Roque Island far to the east in Englishman Bay. Young stopped his truck on a bluff overlooking the beach, and we could see the neighboring island of Criehaven beyond. The island is actually called Ragged Island, but—like the Beatles's song, which has the refrain "everyone knew her as Nancy"—everyone calls Ragged, Criehaven, which is really the name of the little village.

Clayton, who turned out to be a bottomless store of lore and history, had been

Criehaven Harbor: *West Wind* waits for low tide to careen on the cobble beach.

telling me bits and pieces of just about everything on our drive to this windy point. He continued. "Did you know that the Indians called Criehaven *Racketash*? Next, the Anglo-Saxons corrupted it to *Ragged Arse* (you know how those Englishmen love their bathroom humor!). In the end it was shortened to just *Ragged*. The historians think that the mapmaker who worked on that chart was too embarrassed to keep writing *Arse!*

"Did you also know that the poet, Edna St. Vincent Millay, used to summer over there on Criehaven. Wrote a poem about Matinicus, too, called "The Gut." I remember some of it. It goes:

> I thought how off Matinicus the tide
> Came pounding in, came running through the Gut,
> While from the rock the warning whistle cried,
> And Children whimpered, and doors blew shut . . .

"Always gives me goose bumps," he said.

From our vantage point on the bluff we watched seabirds dart and dive. The ball-shaped guillemots seemed to have replaced the thick-necked eiders of farther down east. In the distance I spotted Betsy, Dicken, and Eliza strolling barefoot at the water's edge. I've never learned how to stick two fingers in my mouth to let loose one of those ear-splitting whistles that are useful for hailing three far-away beachcombers. Clayton Young didn't know how to either; instead he said, "Watch this." He cupped his hands and let loose with a most horrific howl. He sounded like a cross between a fog horn and a berserk yodeler. Instantly, three heads popped up and waved in recognition.

By way of explanation, Young told me of the generations-old rivalry between two of the early Matinicus families: the story of the battle to be King of Matinicus, fought between an Ames and a Young.

"Someone decided to settle this dispute once and for all. The King," he said, "would be whoever won a yelling contest. So they climbed Mount Ararat right behind you there, and my ancestor, Grandfather Young, went first, yelling as loud as he possibly could.

"When he was done, Old Man Ames turned to him, astonished, and said, 'You win.' "

We had been told that we would find Monhegan different from Matinicus. Naturally, I thought. Eden and Elysium probably had some differences, too. Ah, but unfortunately the prediction of the resident of Matinicus (into whose forecast I had mentally factored a grain or two of salt) was right on the money.

Once, in Africa, I was riding into Nairobi from Jomo Kenyatta Airport when I saw a bus with a huge sign painted down its entire length:

TOURISTICAL COACH

At first I did not realize what an important—and useful—new word I was learning. *Touristical* looked, and felt, normal on first glance, but it appears in no dictionary of the English language. Some Kikuyu tribesman working in a government bus depot probably painted it there, and I will go to my grave never knowing if he did so out of ignorance of English or because he was the wittiest municipal sign painter in East Africa.

There are times when touristical captures just the perfect flavor of a place, and, try as I might, I can think of no other suitable adjective. This had happened to me when we stopped earlier in Camden, which can be as busy as Stockbridge, Massachusetts, or Sausalito, California, on a summer Saturday. Camden's waterfront attracts tourists like honey does ants.

Monhegan suffers the same affliction. The naysayer on Matinicus *was* right. Monhegan is different, and the reason is that it has become so much more touristical.

We approached the 140-foot high Burnt Head cliffs along the southeastern end of the island. We had caught a gentle morning northwesterly and a fair tide, and the trip had been languid although not disagreeable.

Seen from the sea, the magnificence of the cliffs that rim Monhegan is indisputable. As we drew closer we could see little dots of color on the ridge line. Closer still we could see more and more dots of color all over the cliffs. Worriedly, I asked Betsy to pass me the field glasses. The colored dots were growing bigger, and some of them were starting to move. Feverishly, I seized the binoculars. Dickens swears my voice jumped three octaves when I cried, "Oh my God, they're *people!*

Okay, I'm exaggerating, but Monhegan does make Matinicus seem like a ghost town.

We found a spot to anchor north of Manana between the islands of Smuttynose and Nigh Duck, right where the *Laura B.,* the *Hardy,* and the *Balmy Days II,* three of the boats that bring tourists to Monhegan from the mainland, keep their moorings. We rowed ashore and headed straight for the Monhegan Store where, as Dicken later wrote in *Consolation*'s log, "we got a little groceries for a lot of money." On the walk back to *Hoggie,* we stopped at the Island Spa, a gift shop where Eliza bought postcards to send home. In the shop was a placard, which read in part "If you can't enjoy the natural beauty of this island without *The New York Times,* *THE BOAT LEAVES AT* 11:30 *AND* 4:00." A worthy sentiment with which I wholeheartedly concurred, but I promise you I saw three individuals reading yesterday's *Times* on the porch of the Island Inn.

Monhegan is well-known as a Mecca for artists. Each summer scores of painters move to the island for the season. The artistic tradition is not new. Rockwell Kent's view of Manana in the winter is in the permanent collection of the Metropolitan Museum in New York. George Bellows painted there. More recently, Jamie Wyeth did too. His series of paintings of Orca Bates, the island boy who was born on Manana Island across Herring Gut from Monhegan, have been widely exhibited and published.

Philip Conkling told me that the tourists on Monhegan bothered Wyeth so much that he took to painting *inside* a large cardboard box. Since then he has fled the island, but still returns to Maine each summer. Now he paints on another island, the location of which I am sworn never to reveal.

For all its problems as an artistical and touristical Mecca, Monhegan remains

Rusticators shooting the breeze on Lobster Cove Road, Monhegan. The American flag flies above the cupola of the Island Inn.

naturally unspoiled and beautiful—thanks in large measure to the efforts of a forty-year-old organization known as Monhegan Associates. We took a long hike from the village center out to Black Head on trails maintained by the Associates. The views make it obvious why so many flock there to paint.

On the way back, in the middle of well-named Cathedral Woods, Eliza and I scared a big buck into flight (scaring us in the process, I might add). We had been making plenty of noise chatting and having fun, but, as we turned around a bend on the wooded path, we surprised him. He froze for a second, glared at us, snorted a few times, resumed eating, snorted again, and finally fled down the path at top speed. The sound of his gallop echoed in the forest, and the receding thumpity-thump of his hooves reminded me of the sound effects at the end of a "Lone Ranger" episode.

The stag disappeared amongst the trees. There was something alluring about his need to be alone, and we decided to follow his siren call and leave beautiful but touristical Monhegan in our wake.

Fifteen
A FOREST PRIMEVAL

My father had loaned me a book for the summer. It was called *Westward Bound in the Schooner Yankee* and written by Captain and Mrs. Irving Johnson.

I had met Captain Johnson briefly one evening at the New York Yacht Club. He appeared very frail, and indeed died later the same year. I felt lucky to have met the man I knew better as a robust adventurer through his books and especially through his extraordinary 1929 documentary, *Around Cape Horn,* which depicts some of the most dramatic, hair-raising storm footage I've ever seen.

Johnson was a young buck when he made the film, but the narration was recorded from his perspective as a mature, raspy-voiced old man. Fifty-one years separated the making of the film and the recording of the narration. Irving Johnson, the elder, had a gentle, here's-how-it-was manner reminiscent of an avuncular

Shipboard life: A lazy afternoon in *Consolation*'s cockpit.

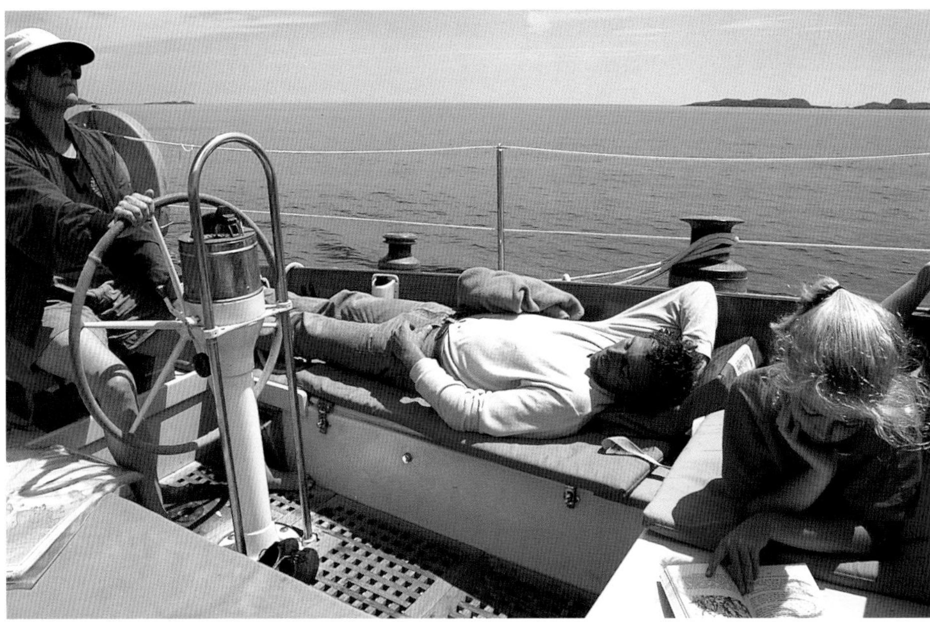

Walter Cronkite type. But Johnson, the younger, was a Johnny Weissmuller character who could perform astonishing feats of athletic prowess every bit as impressive as Tarzan's. The counterpoint works wonderfully.

One of my favorite bits involved the manly sport of sail climbing, a macho sport in which, if you let go, you die. The idea was to lower yourself down the outside edges of the *Peking*'s square-rigged sails using only your thumbs and fingers to grip the canvas. The *Peking,* incidentally, was the largest sailing ship in the world at the time. Each of her four masts supported six square sails adding up to acres of canvas. You had to support your entire body weight with your hands and lower yourself down, hand over hand, sail after sail. No knees, no legs, no feet; those were the rules. "A most insecure feeling," was the way Johnson put it in his narration.

Sailing away from Monhegan, I began reading the Johnsons' book, *Westward Bound.* It describes a circumnavigation of the globe by the 92-foot schooner *Yankee* in the 1930s. It was the first of a series of Captain Johnson adventure books that would span thirty-four years.

Tucked in between two pages was a small sepia-toned photograph of four fit-looking young men on board ship. The fading snapshot was the reason my father had loaned me the book. At the helm in the photograph was, unmistakably, Captain Irving Johnson. Next to him was a grinning fellow in his midtwenties, arms crossed over his bare chest, looking splendidly salty. That, my father's note informed me, was Leverett Davis, childhood friend of his and sailor extraordinaire.

They were neighbors in Fenwick, my family's summer home on the Connecticut shore. Although ten years older, Lev Davis was a friend to my father in the manner of a big brother, and they were bound by their common bond, sailing. It seems that Lev was somewhat of a hero to the boys in Fenwick. There were few races he didn't win. When he signed on with Captain Johnson, his status was elevated higher still.

All this has been by way of explaining why we were steering a course through a light rain to Harbor Island in Muscongus Bay, current home of one Leverett Davis, now seventy-eight years old. I had never met Mr. Davis. He'd left Fenwick decades earlier, and there was no phone to forewarn him. We plowed across Old Hump Channel, Muscongus Bay, anyway, headed for Harbor Island, altogether uninvited.

We eased into the protected anchorage from which the island takes its name. Two boats from nearby Hog Island were ahead of us dropping off thirty or forty young Audubon hikers on a day trip.

The National Audubon Society maintains an extensive nature preserve on Hog, the Todd Wildlife Sanctuary, and at the top of the island operates a summer camp that is probably one of the earliest environmental education centers anywhere. It was founded in 1936, about the same time Lev Davis was crossing oceans on *Yankee.* Hog is also the summer headquarters of our Puffin Project friends, Steve Kress and Evie Weinstein.

On Harbor Island, Davis has given the northern end to the National Audubon Society. It is a favored nesting area for eiders, and there are guillemots and

The forest primeval.

great blue herons as well. It is now called the Duryea Morton Audubon Sanctuary. Nesting ospreys are plentiful on the southern end. On the remaining hundred acres of the island, Davis has donated a "forever wild" conservation easement. His commitment and generosity don't stop there, however. He was a founding director of The Maine Coast Heritage Trust, and, as an island owner, he has donated that most precious of commodities, his solitude. Davis encourages the public to share his beautiful island with him.

We rowed ashore hoping to find him home. Tied to the dock of pilings and stones where we landed was a white double-ended "peapod" dory. No matter how you looked at it, the pristine little craft was perfectly symmetrical: seen both in the fore and aft orientations and mirrored in the still waters of the harbor. It seemed like a metaphor for the serenity of the island and for what I imagined was the well-balanced personality of its owner.

We walked up the path to the house and were told by a friendly caretaker that Mr. Davis had had to depart unexpectedly for the mainland. I was enormously disappointed. We had all been looking forward to meeting him, Betsy and I in particular because we had read the Johnson book. But it was not to be.

We did take advantage of his public-mindedness and hiked around the shore of the island. We saw many osprey nests, their owners angrily kee-ee-ing at us as we passed. We walked through a forest primeval and discovered an eerie cave. On Harbor Island you feel as if *you* are discovering it even though you know that thousands have had the same feeling before you. The beaches are broad, rocky, with a jumbled strata of shists, in which the layers of bedded sediment are arrayed vertically as if they had been turned on their sides. I suppose at some geologic crossroads that is exactly what did happen. Beach roses and beach peas are everywhere, and in crevices among the rocks violet wild asters grow. The only sadness in this surround of beauty is the beating the spruce trees are taking from wind and weather and what Dicken calls "acid fog." We saw frequent blow-downs and widespread damage. Nonetheless, it was truly a magic place.

Returning to *Hoggie* we came across the island's well head. The conservation ethic of Lev Davis was evident even here. A plaque nailed to the top of it read: Well Housing—Designed and Constructed of flotsam and jetsam by Leverett B. Davis, Harbor Island, 1978.

We left Harbor in a light rain.

Not every Friendship sloop ever built was built in Friendship, Maine, but a lot of them were. To me, the Friendship Sloop—more than the wind-jamming schooners, more than the clipper ships (which sailors throughout the world came to call Down Easters), even more than the lobster boats—epitomized all that is

A study in symmetry: A peapod tied up to Harbor Island's dock.

The unusual vertical array of bedded sediment on Harbor's shoreline.

elemental and enduring about Maine shipbuilding. There are not as many Friendships being built today, of course, but of those that are and of those that still ply Maine's waters a lot of them will convene every summer in Friendship.

Friendship Sloop Day is a popular event held annually each July, the sight of which delights owners and on-lookers alike. It has been an annual tradition for thirty consecutive years. Nowhere else can you see such a stirring parade of gracefully-lined sailing boats. From their needle-like bowsprits down the fluid sweep of their sheers to their long booms poking just aft of the transom, they are an ecstasy of form. From their topmasts to their multiple flying headsails—flying jib, inner jib, staysail, jib topsail, yankee—to their gaff-rigged mainsail they are a triumph of function. Once working sailboats, before engines eliminated such a thing, the Friendships were said to be able to "go wherever they pleased." So much so that they were used as light coasting freighters, fishing boats, and even lobster boats. They were that maneuverable, and a central feature of the design was a close-to-the-water gunwale, which made it feasible to haul nets, potwarp, and traps into the cockpit.

We missed this year's Friendship Sloop Day, but paid a visit to the Friendship Museum anyway. The rain was heavier now, and we walked smartly up Friendship's main street in search of the building. It is located in what used to be the schoolhouse and, while hardly a substitute for a gathering of Friendship Sloops, it is nonetheless charming and displays the great pride Friendshippers have for their town and its most famous product.

Near the museum is a sign which seems to express the spirit of the town:

FREEDOM 45
LIBERTY 33
HARMONY 96
UNITY 52
UNION 20
HOPE 27

FRIENDSHIP
IS HERE

The rain cleared as Pemaquid Point disappeared astern. On the starboard beam Thread of Life's bold ledges were visible, but we were well out of harm's way. Closer to us on the same side was one of the many Thrumcap Islands, which dot the coastal waters hereabouts. What evocative names!

Although the residual swells of yesterday's rain squalls rolled underneath us, it was turning into a pleasant day, and the crew was drying out in the cockpit. Later, the day became so sultry, the broadside roll so somnolescent that I fell fast asleep.

Dicken interrupted my midday nap to report that we were nearing Damariscove, which is five miles south of Boothbay Harbor. Our destination was a narrow, nearly treeless island less than two miles long and a scant five hundred yards at its widest point—an island far richer in history, though, than its tiny size would indicate. I felt guilty for not having relieved him, but Dicken, no matter how

Pemaquid Point on a nasty afternoon. The peninsula separates Johns and Muscongus bays.

sleepy, gets as alert as a lynx before making a landfall. There was no point suggesting relief now.

The harbor is a deep inverted U at the southern end of the island. On the chart it looks like a crotch between two chubby thighs. The "old sea" of the last few inclement days continued to batter the steps of the island's southeastern shore. It seemed unlikely that the narrow harbor so exposed to the south would be anything but uncomfortably roll-y, and for a moment I regretted making the offshore trip. But as we rounded the point we could see the top of a mast over the knoll. While the heavy rollers pounded the rocky shore and broke over The Motions in spumes of white, windswept froth, the mast top inside the neck was as steady as an old tree. It was no wonder that seamen had gravitated to Damariscove for as many centuries as they had.

The Indians, of course, were there first. Each year when the weather warmed up, Abanakis (who called Damariscove *Aquahega* or landing place) would paddle out to the island to fish for cod, collect eggs from the vast numbers of eiders, pick berries, and generally bask in the warmth of summer. When the Europeans arrived, at least in the beginning, the Indians would bring produce, hides, and furs to trade with them.

"Damariscove was, from 1608, let us say, to about 1625, the chief maritime port of New England." wrote historian Charles Knowles Bolton in 1929. "Here was the rendezvous for English, French and Dutch ships crossing the Atlantic. Here men bartered with one another and with Indians, drank, gambled, quarreled and sold indentured servants . . ."

The chief maritime port of New England? Here on this tiny, desolate island? It didn't seem possible. But apparently hundreds of years ago this minuscule

The *U*-shaped harbor at isolated Damariscove Island. On the left, the old Coast Guard station, now a private home. *Consolation* is the boat with the more neatly furled sails.

harbor—so slender that we had to set bow and stern anchors to keep from swinging into the shore—was home to no less than thirty cod fishing boats. And freighters for shipping the fish back to the Old Country were frequent visitors.

Indeed, long before the colonies of Plymouth, Jamestown, Popham, and Massachusetts Bay were established, European explorers were fishing for cod in the cornucopic waters off Damariscove. Captain George Popham, whose family gave its name to one of those colonies in 1607, wrote that the plentiful cod were even "bigger and larger fyshe than thay wch coms from the bancke of the New Found Land." So successful was the colony on Damariscove that the Pilgrim settlers at the Plymouth Colony turned to them for emergency assistance. After the first brutal winter at Plymouth when starvation and disease were rife, a colonist named Edward Winslow was dispatched to seek help. He found an abundance of food, supplies, and generosity at Damariscove. And he found that "they would not take any bills for same but did what they could freely."

It is amazing to realize how much older Damariscove is than the other colonies. Countless European seamen had been to Damariscove and back before the *Mayflower* even left Southampton. It is strange, too, to think of a settlement as anonymous as Damariscove bailing out its more famous sister-colony, Plymouth. How many times did we read about Plymouth or Jamestown in grammar school? And how many times did we study the Damariscove Colony? Read about those first few harsh winters? Worry whether the settlers had ample deerskins to keep them warm and enough maize to keep them nourished? I don't know about you, but Damariscove wasn't in *my* social studies book.

In time the fishermen were joined by farmers. Sheep and cows, pigs and chickens were introduced, and in 1882 a Captain Wright bought the island. He

built an icehouse, began to quarry granite, and brought tourism to the island. He renovated the farmhouse with rooms for thirty-five guests, and he constructed three rental units. Two years later he went bust.

In 1939 the last family went back to the mainland. In 1960 the last full-time fisherman left the island, unable or unwilling to stay. For the first time in 350 years this weather-battered island was left with no permanent settlement. All that was left, beside the hilly moors of abandoned scrubland, desolate beauty, and grasses flattened by the wind, were the remains of a remote outpost's few buildings, which had gradually fallen victim to February gales and September hurricanes.

Six years later salvation came through the good offices of the Maine Chapter of the Nature Conservancy. The Conservancy, like its compatriots, the Maine Coast Heritage Trust, the Audubon Society, and the Island Institute, is a major player in the battle to preserve the coast. Elsewhere in Maine the Conservancy has eighty-seven preserves, fifty-five of which are islands. In 1966 it became steward of Damariscove Island.

Each summer two "caretaker/naturalists" are hired by the Conservancy to spend sixteen weeks on the island. When we landed at the remains of the granite pier Captain Wright had built a hundred years earlier, we were greeted by the young couple who had the job this summer. Betsy Banks and Peter Hodum were both Environmental Studies graduates of Bowdoin College. When they told me that, it occurred to me that when I was in college not only did Environmental Studies not exist but rocket scientists were the only people who knew what the "ozone layer" was; no one knew what "global warming" was; and magazines and newspapers routinely had to define the word "ecology."

The Banks-Hodum team were delightful and earnest. From the middle of June until Labor Day, they live in a small shack with neither power nor running water. Their mission is twofold, to protect Damariscove from those who would harm it and to assist those who come to enjoy its remote splendor. They seemed to be enjoying doing both and sad that Labor Day loomed. Most of all they seemed positively thrilled when Betsy thought to invite them for dinner aboard *Consolation.* Meanwhile, we set off on our afternoon round-island expedition.

We didn't often get the chance to host a dinner party and looked forward to it. Cheeseburgers, it turned out, were the dish-of-the-day, and they were cooked to perfection. Dicken later wrote in the ship's log, "Betsy was the burgermeister at the grill, and the cheeseburgers were rare, juicy, and delicious."

We even uncorked a precious bottle of wine, one of three that Betsy had put aside for just such an occasion. It was a tasty Haut-Médoc, a Château Sénéjac, which she had squirreled away in *Consolation*'s temperature-controlled wine cellar—known also as the bilge.

We spent a cozy evening with our new Nature Conservancy friends, and it seemed as if only a few minutes had passed before we decided to open another bottle. Peter, whose plans included a Ph.D. program in environmental issues the following year at the University of California at Davis, told us more of the history of Damariscove.

Turning to Eliza he said, "Most kids growing up in Maine know the story of Captain Patishall. It's kind of a ghost story, but it's true. Do you want to hear it?"

The shack where the Nature Conservancy "caretaker/naturalists" spend the summer.

"Absolutely," she replied without hesitation, although she snuggled a little closer to her Uncle Dicken. It was dark, and the light breeze had backed around to the northwest. Two citronella candles in red glass bowls lit the cockpit, throwing eerie shadows onto the nearby shore. It was a dreamy setting for a spooky story.

"This happened a long time ago back during King Philip's War in the year 1675," Peter began in a quiet voice. "Now you might think that Philip was some kind of English or French or Spanish king, but actually he was the Chief of the Wampanoag Indians. His real name was Metacomet; it was the English who called him King Philip because he was a brave man and a fierce warrior and they were a little afraid of him.

"History books are a shade vague on this part of the story: It seems that King Philip went to Plymouth and pledged to maintain friendly relations with the English, but, as usual, the colonists welshed on their side of the bargain. This made King Philip really mad. He gathered his tribe together and they raided English villages in Damariscotta, Arrowsic, Sheepscot, and Pemaquid. At one point people were so scared that nearly three hundred of them came here to be safe. Most of them left, but a few remained. Soon a band of Indians in war canoes came here and burned down the houses and cut the throats of the cattle. They stole a sloop and killed one person."

Eliza stared at Peter with gratifyingly wide eyes.

"At this time a Captain Richard Patishall owned Damariscove. He wasn't on the island when this happened, though. He was on his sloop in Pemaquid. That night an Indian raiding party slipped aboard his boat, which was probably a lot like this one. And they murdered him with knives and tomahawks. Then the Indians

chopped his head off, which showed that they respected him as a worthy adversary. They threw his body overboard and kept his head. His loyal dog couldn't bear to be parted from his master. So he dove in after him, but the water was so cold and rough that he drowned.

"After a while it is said that his body and that of his faithful dog fetched up on the shore of *this very island,* where the two of them had lived so happily before.

"To this very day on a moonlit night you can sometimes see the headless body of poor Captain Patishall walking on that bluff right over there. His dog always follows him, a ghostly but trusty companion. Sometimes, when the wind is right, I wake up in the middle of the night only to hear his mournful and immortal baying. . . ."

As we prepared for bed, the light northwesterly was not the only chill in the air. Eliza started off the night in her mother's bunk.

We stopped briefly in Boothbay Harbor for provisions. We had run out of nearly everything. Boothbay is a bustling resort town, which boasts five municipal parking lots, an around-town trolley that runs every half hour, and fifty daily harbor cruises, one of which is Cap'n Fish's Sightseeing Cruise aboard the *Pink Lady.* I noticed in the official Boothbay Harbor Region Chamber of Commerce Directory that there is a bed and breakfast called A Site To Sea ("a nonsmoking establishment"), a guest house called The Maine Idea ("no pets"), and an inn called The Sleepy Lobsterman ("your hosts, Dottie and Earl"). The Fisherman's Wharf Inn at Pier 6 claims to be "Innfamous, Innspirational, Inntimate, Innviting, And Inncomparable." Boothbay seemed to embody all the ticky-tack and honky-tonk that makes Route 1 so depressing, and it's not even *on* Route 1. I feared I would not like it very much.

We tied up at a long fuel dock with the inauspicious name Carousel Marina, Ltd. One of the problems of cruising in popular areas like Boothbay Harbor is that dock space is a precious commodity. The marina generally wants to refuel you and get you on your way as quickly as possible. The name Carousel strongly suggested that sort of scenario.

The uniformed pump jockey just about jumped to attention when we made fast. "Fill 'er up? Diesel? Need any water? Ice? Need to go grocery shopping?"

"Whoa, slow down," I said. "We do need to go to the supermarket. But can we stay here for a while?"

"Of course." Big smile. "You can tie up here as long as you like. We'll look after your boat. Don't worry about a thing." Wait a minute. Was I hearing him correctly?

We walked up to the marina-office/yacht-chandlery where a gray-haired woman, also in uniform, advised us that the big, inexpensive supermarket was really too far for walking. "Why don't you borrow our car?" she said. Borrow your car? Had I died and gone to marina heaven?

My advice to you: If you ever sail into Boothbay Harbor in need of food, fuel, ice, water, friendship, *anything,* make a beeline for the Carousel Marina. It's part way down Spruce Point on the eastern side of the harbor. You can't go wrong.

Sixteen

FIFTY-FIVE FEET, SEVEN INCHES

Consolation, responsive and eager, knifed across Boothbay Harbor. Meanwhile, an ambitious plan was afoot to navigate what is known as The Inside Passage—a thirty-eight-mile inland voyage from Boothbay to Bath and (after an overnight stop in Merrymeeting Bay) down the mighty Kennebec River to its mouth.

While I steered through the jumble of boats moored in Boothbay Harbor, Dicken and Betsy pored over *Eldridge Tide and Pilot,* the *Tidal Current Tables,* and the most detailed chart we had aboard. There was more to this adventure than met the eye. As our trusty copilot, the Taft cruising guide, warned, "The Inside Passage is one of the adventures of the Maine coast. Like marriage, however, it is not to be entered into lightly, but advisedly . . . and soberly. The current in two of the stretches, Upper and Lower Hell Gates, can be awesome for those not accustomed to running white-water rivers in deep-keeled boats."

The trip itself would take us through eighteen distinct bodies of water. We would meander along rivers and through guts and passages and back channels and across smooth-surfaced, lake-like bays. It would be our first taste of Maine's interior. Dicken gave us an oral itinerary. To Eliza's amusement, he had to turn the chart every which way but upside down in order to read the names along the route. The complexity of the expedition clearly delighted both of them.

"Listen to this," he said. "This is going to be great. After we clear Juniper Point at the mouth of Boothbay Harbor, we head up Townsend Gut, pass the swing bridge and cross the Sheepscot River. It's about a mile and three-quarters wide there. Then we dip through Goose Rock Passage, pass the entrance to Robinhood Cove, cross Knubble Bay, and then we're in the Sasanoa River. Just before Hockomock Bay we have to pass through S-shaped Lower Hell Gate. That's our first problem area.

"In Hockomock Bay we cross the Back River. After that we're back in the Sasanoa. Halfway to Hanson Bay we have to get through Upper Hell Gate. That's our second problem area, but worse than the first.

"Then there's a bridge at Arrowsic. Wait a second. . . . Uh-oh."

"What's that supposed to mean?" I asked, unaccustomed to Dicken saying "uh-oh."

"It says on the chart that the bridge's high water clearance is fifty-one feet. D'you know how tall our mast is?"

"I *think* it's fifty-five feet, seven inches," I said. Uh-oh.

Dicken sloughed off this apparent mismatch. "We'll just go under at low tide."

Being the more cautious of the two, I would need to give that little anomaly a second or two more thought, particularly since we could no longer take advantage of the extreme tidal drops we had seen farther down east.

When I was a child, the man who lived in the house behind ours in Fenwick, an experienced sailor, bought a restored two-masted schooner. He and his cronies threw a big maiden voyage party at the Essex Yacht Club before shoving off for their first cruise. Apparently the party was too much of a success. When they reached the drawbridge at the mouth of the Connecticut River, they forgot to wait for it to open. Passing underneath it, all sails flying, they sheared off both masts, nearly killing themselves in the bargain.

Unperturbed, Dicken continued: "After the bridge, we head up the Kennebec River past Bath, jog around Lines Island up the West Branch, through Goose Cove and the Chop and finally into Merrymeeting Bay. "What a great name! Merrymeeting Bay. Look at the chart, it's amazing. Five different rivers come together there: the Androscoggin, Abagadasset, Cathance, Kennebec, and the Muddy. And guess what, Eliza? I'll bet the water that far inland will be w-a-r-m!"

But before we would reach water you could actually swim in, even before that too-low bridge at Arrowsic Island, there were the two Hell Gates we needed to worry about. The object was to hit them at high slack water, which, to complicate matters, is not the same as high tide. And the trick is deciding when that will be.

We had the Cobscook Reversing Falls under our belt, so we knew that we would have to interpolate considerably from the times the tide tables list just to calculate high tide. In other words, if *Eldridge* says that high tide in Boothbay for this particular August morning will be at 11:16 A.M., then we have to estimate how much *later* it will be six miles up river. Then there is the difficulty of estimating the deviation between high tide and *high slack water,* that brief interval between flood and ebb when the current quiets enough to make a Hell Gate passable. If you've been clever (or lucky) enough, you should be *following* the elusive moment of slack as you and it move inland.

The first thing we saw upon entering Goose Rock Passage was a shipwreck. Unafraid, we ignored it. Based on all our laborious calculations we thought we had the timing right, and we proceeded under power toward Lower Hell Gate. The current there is controlled by the differing water levels of the two great rivers it joins: the Sheepscot to the east and the Kennebec to the west. At the height of an ebbing tide the current can run eight knots, which would overwhelm an auxiliary engine like *Consolation*'s.

We felt proud that our careful planning had paid off. We slipped though Lower Hell Gate with a minimum of fuss. At Upper Hell Gate we were again nicely in sync with slack water, but the current there was apparently spirited all the time. *Consolation* yawed and slipped, and I had a deuce of a time steering through. I had visions of doing a one-eighty and getting flushed out backwards.

Overleaf

Two reminders of an era past: the decaying wrecks of the four-masted schooners, *Luther Little* and *Hesper.* I had no intention of joining them.

Suddenly, the Gate got very narrow—maybe fifty yards wide from bank to bank. I was so close to the muddy bank at one point, I thought we would fetch up on it.

But we didn't, and in no time we were anchored in a tranquil bay surrounded by marshland. Dicken recapped the day in *Consolation*'s log, "The tide and current performed roughly as predicted in that we seemed to be a little behind or a little ahead of slack the whole way." He also included a description of the abundant wildlife thereabouts: "We watched the tide fall exposing a grassy-banked, meandering expanse of mud. Lesser yellow-legs, little blues, least sandpipers, and semipalmated plovers populated the marsh. Kingfishers and ospreys, bluefish and cormorants all broke the shimmery surface."

The Max L. Wilder Bridge is named for a former Maine State Highway Commissioner. It links Arrowsic Island and the town of Woolwich, and it spans the Sasanoa, at the place where that river meets the Kennebec. From our anchorage in Hanson Bay we could see the city of Bath under the span of the bridge.

You would have thought it was the Bridge over the River Kwai, we spent so much time analyzing it. The chart was, however, unequivocal on one point: At high water the center of the span is fifty-one feet *exactly*. *Consolation*'s mast is fifty-five feet, seven inches, *exactly*, and that doesn't count the VHF antenna. We opted to spend the night at Hanson Bay. What could be prettier? What could be safer?

The tide table for Bath said that low tide would occur at 8:00 A.M., but we were up hours in advance. During breakfast we double-checked the tables and kept a weather eye on the clock. Moronically, we watched the level of the water fall against the granite pilings of the bridge. It was boring work.

Suddenly, although it was still only 6:30 A.M., I got this idiotic idea that I could sight the mast height if I climbed up onto the bridge. Ignoring all efforts at reason, I jumped into *Hoggie* and rowed ashore by myself. I tied up at a small rowboat float near the base of the bridge. There were two or three half-derelict dinghies also tied to the float; none had been bailed since the last rainstorm. Or else they were leaking. Up a short, overgrown path there was a picket fence with a locked gate. The fence was easily jumpable, which is exactly what I did.

The early morning tranquillity was wrecked by the sound of squealing tires braking on asphalt. It was my first indication that I wasn't alone. Nervously, I looked around. At the end of the dead-end road there was a red Chevrolet where, seconds ago, there had been nothing. An enormous red-faced man was struggling to get out.

"Who the hell you think you are, trespassing my property?" he shouted.

Granted, there *had* been a No Trespassing sign next to the locked gate. I had been warned, but he certainly seemed to be overreacting.

He was a mean looking guy, thick-necked and really huge. In his right hand he had two oarlocks. Maybe I'm crazy, but I could have sworn he was holding them like makeshift brass knuckles.

Something Mick Jagger once said popped uninvited into my head: "It's all right letting yourself go, as long as you can let yourself back." I hoped this guy wasn't going to let go any farther.

A great blue heron in Hockomock Bay along The Inside Passage.

"You want to know who owns this place?" he spat. (I still hadn't said a word.) "I own this place, is who. So get the hell outta here!"

What I really wanted to say was *up thine with turpentine, pal,* and toss in the one-fingered salute for good measure, but instead I thought I'd first try the reasonable approach.

"Since I'm already here, would you mind if I left my boat for just a couple of minutes? I just need to go up to the bridge. . . ." It sounded lame even to my ears.

To my utter astonishment his whole demeanor changed. It was as if a chain saw had suddenly run out of gas. He let out a deep sigh, turned away from me, and said, almost to himself, "Well, since you've already committed the crime, I don't see much sense in throwing you out now." I wasted no time climbing up onto the Max L. Wilder Bridge and putting some distance between me and this maniac.

When I got to the middle of the span, I could have jumped off. What a waste! I couldn't tell if *Consolation*'s mast was above, below, or even with the bridge. It was impossible to judge. And to think I'd been nearly beaten to death by an enraged property owner wielding oarlocks.

Back aboard *Consolation,* tide-watching had become an all-hands task now that the ships's chronometer read 0743. Betsy and Dicken went forward to haul the anchor aboard. I got into *Hog Wild* and rowed ahead to station myself right under the bridge. We had decided that it would be impossible to gauge whether the mast would hit the bridge looking up from the deck. I would be the final judge with the benefit of a distant perspective.

The tide was ebbing strongly against *Consolation* as Dicken nosed her upstream toward the bridge. From where I stood in the tender, it looked like it was going to be extremely close to call. The rest of the crew all stood on deck like tourists at the bottom of the World Trade Center. *Consolation* powered closer. I checked my digital watch—7:59. Dicken had set the throttle for just a hair more power than the current he was bucking. The bow had already gone under the span; the mast had just a few yards. I had to make a decision. Dicken looked over at me and gave his shoulders a shrug. I thought it was still too close to call, but I was determined not to be a party to the dismasting of *Consolation.* I was just about to give the abort signal, when I saw Dicken lean over and reach for the throttle. It could mean only one thing: He agreed and had decided to slow the speed. He would then drift back on the current out of danger.

Or so I thought.

Dicken, who has the daring of the first man to eat an oyster, instead *increased* the speed. As *Consolation*'s mast went under the bridge, I watched her VHF antenna flick along the bottom of the bridge's superstructure. Whew!

Due west lay the river city of Bath, a focal point of Maine shipbuilding, past and present. The Bath Iron Works, Maine's largest employer, dominates the waterfront. A short hop to the south, the Maine Maritime Museum now occupies the original site of the Percy & Small Shipyard.

No longer the principal business of the Maine coast, the shipbuilding industry has, however, survived remarkably well over the years through adaptability and

We opted to spend the night at Hanson Bay. What could be prettier? What could be safer?

CONSOLATION

good old Yankee ingenuity. It began with the hardy and robust little thirty-tonner, the Popham Colony's *Virginia.* After her Kennebec River launching in 1607, she plied the coast trading in furs, cod, and sassafras root, spent two decades transporting tobacco between Virginia and England, and reached her demise shipwrecked off the coast of Ireland.

In the years before the outbreak of the American Civil War, shipbuilding and Maine became synonymous. Between then and now, more ships have been launched from Bath than from any comparable strip of waterfront anywhere in the world.

Indeed, Maine's supremacy in the art and craft of shipbuilding was global. The slogan "Bath-built" was recognized and respected throughout the world. The great clipper ship *Flying Dragon* sailed from Bath around the Horn to San Francisco in a stunning ninety-seven days. The Down Easter, *Wandering Jew,* holds

The Bath Iron Works on the Kennebec River. The red-and-white striped crane, "Number 11," is the tallest in the Western world.

The Max L. Wilder Bridge and *Consolation* meet. Nearly.

the San Francisco–Hong Kong record to this day; she flew across the Pacific in thirty-three days.

Today the Bath Iron Works is again in a period of economic flux after a volatile history, which includes two bankruptcies and a devastating fire. I don't know if BIW's motto remains viable ("Ahead of schedule and under budget!") since its principal client is the United States Navy, but as a taxpayer I hope so. Great warships on the scale of guided missile frigates and the like are still built at Bath. As we motored slowly by, we gawked at a recently launched cruiser. It not only towered above the mast top of *Consolation,* but it dwarfed the Max L. Wilder Bridge, too.

It would be no exaggeration to say that the Bath Iron Works has been indispensable to this country's war efforts since the outbreak of the Spanish-American War, which began eight years after General Thomas Hyde founded BIW in 1890. Remember the *Maine?* During the Second World War, for example, the Bath Iron Works built more destroyers than the entire Japanese Navy.

Ships of less destructive capacity were included in BIW's proud roster too: Ships built for speed like Vanderbilt's J-Class *Ranger,* which successfully defended the 1937 America's Cup. (It is interesting to note that *every* member of the first America's Cup Team came from Maine.) And there were ships built for more decadent pursuits like J. P. Morgan's 343-foot yacht *Corsair,* the one which prompted Morgan's famous reply when asked how much she cost: "If you have to ask, you can't afford one."

Downstream at Percy & Small some forty-one schooners were built between 1897 and 1920. Some had four masts, some five, and a few *six;* the *Wyoming* (with six) was the largest wooden sailing ship ever built—a sort of seagoing Spruce Goose. Later Percy & Small launched the *Thomas W. Lawson.* Her hull constructed entirely of steel, she was the only seven-masted schooner ever made.

A friend of Betsy's brother Coe, Hannah Batchelder, who is a Maine Maritime Museum volunteer, led us through the original Percy & Small shipyard buildings with such evocative names as the Mold Loft, the Mill and Joiners' Shop, the Paine and Treenail Shop, and the Caulker's Shed. Like the WoodenBoat School in Brooklin, MMM supports an Apprenticeship program, which teaches the art and craft of wooden boat construction and restoration and seeks to keep alive the true spirit of Maine shipbuilding. I briefly interrupted the work of Conrad Feder, an apprentice from Fairbanks, Alaska. He described the one-year program as enormously valuable but admitted that he was tired of being on display.

"We're meant to be part actor, part physical display, and part work force," he said. The apprentices work while the public watches and one week out of every eight (there are eight apprentices) they act as "interpreter," an unpopular job that involves answering the questions of nosy tourists like myself.

Feder was hard at work on the restoration of a Northeast One-Design sloop, the *Thetis.* It would be some time before *Thetis* could be re-launched; much loving work remained, much elbow-grease was still to be done. Feder had nailed a sign above his work area. It seems clear it held some secret irony for him. It said: "Live and work in places tourists only visit."

Chief instructor Phil Shelton helps apprentice Bill Wright at the Maine Maritime Museum's Apprenticeshop.

Warships, freighters, coasters, and clippers—ships of every size and description—have slipped down the ways on Bath's waterfront. For many years the launching tradition has been to smash a bottle of champagne across the bows by way of christening her and wishing her luck. But in the old days rum was the liquor of choice—and not only as a liquid to be squandered on ceremony.

It seems that the consumption of rum and the building of ships were inextricably linked for the Maine man of the nineteenth century. Rum, an inexpensive commodity of trade with the West Indies, was rationed by yard owners to their workers in a manner that would force an OSHA inspector of today into premature retirement.

Early on a cold morning shortly after arriving at work, the men would be issued their first ration of the day: a full tumbler of rum, two full tumblers of water (optional). By the time eleven o'clock rolled around, a little midmorning pick-me-up was dispensed. And the four o'clock distribution saw the men over the rocky shoals of the afternoon's endeavors. Naturally, any punctuation point in the construction of the ship—nailing the last plank of the deck, for example—called for a work-stopping, rum-snorting celebration. It was only during the launching of a ship that the rum was wasted.

We left the "City of Ships" with the strong sense that Bath's nickname was not a meaningless boast. We flew up the Kennebec on a fair tide, flying just the genoa. In no time we were in another world: Merrymeeting Bay. Gone were the spruce, the balsam, and Jewett's "pointed firs." This is a land of rolling farms and brackish water warm enough to swim in, a place where marshes replace the rocky headlands and where so many migrating waterfowl are attracted that it has become a sportsman's paradise.

We searched the eastern edge of the bay for a suitable place to spend the night. Betsy said, out of the blue, why not here? At that precise instant two fledgling bald eagles took to the air in a dramatic flurry. Dicken and I looked at one another. Yes, here. I dropped the anchor.

We spent the late afternoon swinging from the spinnaker halyard and frolicking in the warm, muddy river water. It was fresh enough to wash in. Each of us in turn borrowed a squirt of Dicken's liquid soap and "Bronnerized." It felt utterly un-Maine—more like a stop in an out-of-the-way Caribbean cove. It was quiet, peaceful, and balmy.

Clean and dry we gathered in the cockpit for a sunset cocktail, and I wondered vaguely what possible advantages Manhattan could have over Merrymeeting Bay. Nightlife you might say, for one. Well, we have some pretty entertaining evening activities aboard *Consolation:* some of the finest cuisine available on land or sea, some rum to drink in the spirit of our Caribbean detour, and no television to pollute our minds. But our favorite after-dinner activity was tuning in Camden Marine on the VHF radio.

Camden Marine is a radio-telephone service for mariners (its corporate name is Coastal Communications). Camden operators patch your radio call to a conventional land line so you can call your mother and tell her that you'll be late for dinner. The only difference between using a telephone and Camden Marine is that every other boat can hear both sides of the conversation. Working boats tend to use the service only for important messages, but the vast majority of Camden Marine customers are pleasure boating summer-types whose mothers, wives, brothers don't have VHF radios in their kitchens the way fishermen's families do.

Camden's operators are famous for their politeness and patience. Many of their customers are radio neophytes and tend to panic with the unfamiliar microphone in their hands. Nearly every call begins with the nervous remark, "I never know how much to say on these things."

From that moment on, the calls take one of two paths: Some continue blandly, like a dull postcard. ("Are you having a good time?" "Yeah, we're having a great time." "Great." "How's the weather been?" "Okay." "Well we better go, this is getting expensive.") But most calls get surprisingly intimate within minutes.

A good example occurred that evening in Merrymeeting Bay. I call this little radio drama "The Alibi:"

SHE: How much can I say on this thing?
HE: Well, what is it that you want to tell me? Remember, everyone can hear what both of us say.

SHE: The thing is, Frankie, I've some bad news for you. You've been busted. They found the dope.

HE: [after some serious radio silence] Oh, God. Listen, honey? Listen up, okay? I've really been missing you, cause *I've been on the boat for three weeks.*

SHE: But, Frankie, no you haven't. You only left on Saturday. . . .

We've eavesdropped on other radio moments courtesy of Camden Marine. We have heard an on-air marriage proposal, a heated discussion about the moral dilemma of using an air conditioner, and this, my all-time favorite, of the man radioing his wife:

HE: Honey, the weather's bad; I can't possibly make it back tonight.

SHE: Okay, dear, but please be careful.

HE: Will do, don't worry. 'Bye, hon.

SHE: 'Bye, dear, see you tomorrow.

HE: Uh, Camden Marine, I'd like to place another call. The number's 555-3246. [pause] Hi, darling, this is Larry. I'm free tonight. . . .

Dicken decided to call his girlfriend Tobie that night to tell her he missed her. So hooked on the pleasures of Camden Marine, Betsy and I made some polite pretense of puttering around with other matters but eavesdropped just the same. And in case you think that the Camden Marine operators are too jaded to listen in, think again. At the end of the call Tobie said, "Oh, and be sure to send my love to the Camden Marine Operator."

This Camden operator, who happened to be a man (most are women), broke in and said, "*Consolation,* are you through with your call?"

"Yes, Camden Marine," Dicken said. "Thank you for your help. this is *Consolation.* We're clear and standing by on Channel 9."

"Thank you for your call, *Consolation,* and Camden sends love back to Tobie. Camden clear."

Against the objections of all hands, I insisted we stop (in the rain) on Eagle Island, where Admiral Robert E. Peary lived his last years. I've always felt rather sorry for poor Admiral Peary. He risked his life (as did his faithful companions, theirs) reaching 90° N. Lat., and then that dreadful Dr. Cook claimed he'd reached the North Pole one year earlier. It was like that woman who started the Boston Marathon, slipped into the MTA, and crossed the finish line first. Even after Cook's claim was generally discredited, detractors sniped for decades that Peary had faked his location. Maybe he *was* only at 89° 57′ N. Lat. But give the poor guy a break, I say. R.I.P., Admiral Peary, you deserve more.

While Dicken and Eliza mutinously stayed aboard *Consolation,* Betsy and I visited Eagle. The house is charming with splendid views of Casco Bay. Built in 1904 and reconstructed in 1912 with architectural details parodying the lines and features of a square-rigger, it reminded me of Warren and Wetmore's New York Yacht Club design. Although he was born in Pennsylvania, Peary was an 1877

Seguin Island Light off Popham Beach. A private group, The Friends of Seguin, work to preserve it.

graduate of Bowdoin in nearby Brunswick, and he spent the last nine years of his life on Eagle. Among all the bric-a-brac and souvenirs an admiral ought to have collected, there is in the living room a photograph taken at (or near) the North Pole. Six men stand shoulder to shoulder swaddled in mukluks and fur-fringed hoods. Eginwah, Ootah, Ooqueh, and Seegloo were the four remaining Eskimos. (The expedition began with twenty-two.) Matthew Henson, a black man, was Peary's assistant and had accompanied him on all the previous expeditions. There in the center of the picture was Peary himself. The only participants missing from the photograph were the forty sled dogs that had mushed Peary to the Pole.

On that triumphant April day in 1909, Admiral Peary wrote this entry in his journal: "The Pole at last!!! The prize of three centuries, my dream and ambition for twenty-three years. Mine at last." What a feeling it must have been.

Seventeen

THE JEWEL BY THE SEA

POUND OF TEA ISLAND GUARDS the mouth of the Harraseeket River in the upper reaches of Casco Bay. This tiny island, I am told, was purchased from Indians for? Can you guess? Right, a pound of tea.

If you should ever find yourself at Pound of Tea with the urge to strike your own bargain, quickly sidestep the island and head up the Harraseeket River to South Freeport. Call for Deb Payzant's taxi and continue by road for three miles up Pine Street to Freeport. There you will find recent economic growth so explosive that the expression "born to shop" takes on unparalleled new meaning. An Elysian field of factory outlets, a Nirvana of name-brand outlets, a paradise of price reduction, a Valhalla of vendors, Freeport is now home to some one hundred plus factory-owned stores and boutiques. A stroll down Route 1 (the Main Street of Freeport) is imperative if shopping is your thing.

One hand casually on the wheel and the other gesturing as she spoke, Deb Payzant explained how sleepy Freeport metamorphosed into its current incarnation as the shoppers' mecca. Lured by extraordinary tax inducements (e.g. tax-exempt status for the first three years), retailers like Ralph Lauren, Brooks Brothers, Calvin Klein, Laura Ashley, Benetton, Mikasa, Dansk, Patagonia, J. Crew, Nike, London Fog, and even the underwear outlet, Olga's, migrated to Freeport like ducks heading north in the spring. In the same way that filling stations cluster at a busy intersection and that you can never find a Burger King without tripping over a McDonald's, they descended on Freeport to be next door to the undisputed king of factory outlets, L.L. Bean, which—fear not—is still open twenty-four hours a day, 365 days a year.

One half of the population of the United States received the L.L. Bean catalog last year, and mail order sales still account for 88 percent of the business. Writing in *Sports Illustrated,* John Skow found the perfect simile: "It's as if L.L. Bean were family, some sort of mildly eccentric but amiable uncle who lives up in Maine and sends us packages."

On the site of the original Ervin and L.L. Bean dry-goods emporium in Freeport, L.L. Bean has had its sole retail store since . . . well, since soles were its only business. The Maine Hunting Shoe started it all in 1912. Leon Leonwood

Bean, tired of wet feet on hunting trips, built a shoe "as light as a pair of moccasins, with the protection of a heavy hunting boot." Ironically, it was this first product that was nearly the company's undoing. The rubber soles kept pulling away from the leather uppers. Ninety of the first hundred pairs sold were returned, but L.L. Bean had an eccentric corporate philosophy: He guaranteed everything he sold, and he never forgot his original retailing credo, "Treat your customers like human beings, and they'll always come back for more."

Leon Gorman, the fifty-seven-year-old current president, wrote about his grandfather, "To hear that one of his products failed was a genuine shock to his system. He'd charge around the factory trying to find an explanation. Then he'd write the customer, return his money, enclose a gift, invite him fishing or do anything else to make the matter right." The rest, as they say, is history. I still have a pair of Bean boots, don't you?

Today, L.L. Bean ranks number two among Maine's tourist attractions; number one is the Atlantic Ocean. Last year the company came close to topping $600 million in sales; the phone bill for their 800 number was $5 million; and on their busiest *day* they shipped 133,700 packages.

The serenity of South Freeport's harbor on the Harraseeket River gives no hint of the shopping mania going on in nearby Freeport.

In spite of all that success, the store is a relative sea of tranquillity amidst the hustle and bustle of Freeport shopping. There is even an indoor trout pond to soothe the consumer's mind. Of course, in the old days it was a great deal quieter. Eliza's fourth grade teacher, Sue Hooker, remembered stopping there many years ago in the middle of a cold winter night. She had been driving since early morning and arrived in Freeport at 3:00 A.M. When she walked in, the only person in sight was an elderly salesman. He was fast asleep in a rocking chair, his feet propped up on an up-ended barrel in front of a pot-bellied stove. He woke up as she approached and said, "Where have you been? I've been waitin' for you all night."

Strange events have taken place there, too. One New Year's Eve a couple arrived shortly before midnight with a justice of the peace in tow. To the delight of customers and staff alike, he married them on the main staircase in the middle of the store.

Today, L.L. Bean ranks number two among Maine's tourist attractions; number one is the Atlantic Ocean.

I once photographed the television talk-show host, Sally Jessy Raphaël (the one with the red spectacles) for a magazine cover, and she too had an L.L. Bean story. She and her husband were touring Maine by car when a serious hurricane threatened. The governor ordered low-lying coastal areas evacuated, and emergency shelters were set up in high school gymnasiums.

"I *refuse* to spend the night on the floor of a gym!" Raphaël told her husband Karl.

"But we have to go *somewhere,*" Karl replied, sensibly. "We'll be arrested if we don't, and there isn't enough time to drive home."

"I've got an idea. . . ."

She headed straight for that irreproachable symbol of stability in a turbulent world: L.L. Bean. With the amused permission of the night manager, she picked out a tent, which was being displayed on the showroom floor, two sleeping bags, and two camp cots. Sally and Karl climbed into the tent, zipped up the door, and spent the night safely indoors courtesy of the world's largest outdoor outfitter.

The "Jewel by the Sea" is the way Henry Wadsworth Longfellow remembered Portland in his poetic memoir, "My Lost Youth." Portland was Longfellow's boyhood home, and one can still visit the house where he lived with his grandparents. In fact it has become something of a literary shrine. It is also headquarters of the Maine Historical Society. From my own school days the Longfellow poem I best remember is the hauntingly beautiful, "The Wreck of the Hesperus." If you've ever read it, surely you remember one of these spooky stanzas:

It was the schooner Hesperus,
        That sailed the wintry sea;
And the skipper had taken his little daughter,
        To bear him company.

He wrapped her warm in his seaman's coat
        Against the stinging blast;
He cut a rope from a broken spar,
        And bound her to the mast.

Portland: "The jewel by the sea."

"Oh father! I see a gleaming light,
Oh say, what may it be?"
But the father answered never a word,
A frozen corpse was he.

At daybreak, on the bleak sea-beach,
A fisherman stood aghast,
To see the form of a maiden fair,
Lashed close to a drifting mast.

Such was the wreck of the Hesperus,
In the midnight and the snow!
Christ save us all from a death like this,
On the reef of Norman's Woe!

I could not help feeling an eerie chill from this poem. It was, after all, about a father taking his young daughter to sea on a trip she does not survive. For me it was all the creepier because Longfellow had based the poem on the true story of a schooner named the *Helen Eliza.*

The demise of the real *Helen Eliza* is a pretty weird story too. During The Great Storm of 1869 she foundered on a ledge near Peaks Island off Portland in Casco Bay. The only survivor was a young man rescued from drowning by the brave men of Peaks Island. One year earlier this same sailor had been the only survivor of a sailing ship that had gone down in a West Indian hurricane. (I was reminded of the fellow we had met in Stonington, Tim Brown, who had also survived two sinkings in the same year.) If there was ever an occasion for discretion being the better part of valor, this was it. To avoid a third, possibly fatal, wreck, our friend from the *Helen Eliza* decided to leave the high seas for good. He bought a farm, safely inland in New Hampshire. There was one more thing he should have done, however; he should have taken swimming lessons. Although he was finally out of reach of the tempestuous Atlantic, he was crossing a small stream on his property when he slipped off a slippery plank, fell in, and drowned.

The city of Portland has had its share of calamity as well. It has twice been completely devastated by fire, once in 1775 and again on July 4, 1866. Reputedly the latter fire was accidentally started by a simple firecracker during festivities

Ruin and rehabilitation: The South Portland waterfront.

celebrating the end of the Civil War. The Portland parks system—there are twenty-six parks in all—was a direct benefit of the Fire of 1866. The park lands, which of course had tremendous potential commercial value, were safeguarded from development by visionary town fathers for "the protection against the spread of fire and [how farsighted they were!] to promote the general health."

Today so many trees shelter the streets and parks of Portland that it is sometimes known as the Forest City. That and its siting between hilly farmland and the temperature-tempering effect of Casco Bay make it a most attractive and comfortable northern New England city. I like to think of it also as a "human scale" city; the buildings are low, the sky always visible, nearby islands are the suburbs, and the panoramic view from the Portland Observatory atop Munjoy Hill is simply splendid.

Eliza and I ate breakfast at an all-purpose diner—the kind of place where you can order everything from fried eggs to crab rolls and lobsters. A sign behind the counter said "The lobster that we serve this day spent last night in Casco Bay." We had eggs and bacon, however, and took a taxi up Munjoy Hill. After climbing the 104 steps to the 360-degree lookout at the top of the observatory, we watched as dozens of small ferries darted hither and thither like little worker bees between the populated islands of Casco Bay and downtown Portland. Riding these ferries are commuters—modern day Mainers who have exchanged their oilskins for business suits, their ditty bags for attaché cases, and are probably more concerned with lobster futures than lobster pots.

The Observatory was built in 1807. Using an elaborate system of code flags, Captain Lemuel A. Moody used it to alert ship owners and the families of crew members to the arrival of ships. From this same tower you have before you a complete picture of this deep-water harbor. One hundred and sixteen miles closer to Europe than any other major northeastern port, Portland's waterfront still bustles. Ferries, draggers, lobster boats, freighters, cruise ships crisscross day and night. When the M/S *Scotia Prince* departs Portland for Yarmouth, Nova Scotia, each evening, you won't see more wattage unless you go to Times Square. At the foot of Munjoy Hill the scarlet-sided lightship *Nantucket* is moored, open to the public. Behind it, arrayed semicircularly around Casco Bay are half a dozen forts, which you can also visit. The Bath Iron Works has an outpost here, too, a floating dry-dock big enough to accommodate a Navy cruiser. Across the harbor entrance in South Portland are docks big enough for those massive container ships. They always look so overloaded and top-heavy that they will roll over and turn turtle, but I guess they don't. Beyond the container ship wharves the first lighthouse ever built in Maine can be seen on Cape Elizabeth. Portland Head Light was first lit in 1791 using sixteen whale oil lamps; President George Washington personally appointed its first keeper, Captain Joseph Greenleaf. And if you look out the back side of the Portland Observatory you can see, on a clear day, the White Mountains dominating the northwest horizon.

If Union Wharf were in any other city besides Portland, only rats would consider living there. A line of makeshift buildings, made of corrugated metal siding and roofs, stretch along the pier. They face a derelict nineteenth-century loft building. Its windows have been sealed shut with cinder blocks; chunks of the brick façade have simply dropped to the ground. In the U of the two piers where the cul-de-sac of water ends, there is a floating dock, the home of the lobster boat

---

Twin lighthouses guide mariners into Portland Harbor from the south. Portland Head Light (foreground) was first lit in 1791 using sixteen whale oil lamps; it is the oldest lighthouse in the nation. A series of nautical disasters forced the construction of Ram Island Ledge Light in 1904.

Eeyore. Fifty-five gallon drums, full of bait, line the top of the dock. Scores of sea gulls battle for the scraps. The sign fastened to the gray corrugated wall admonishes:

Authorized Boats Only
No Rafting
No Dumping
No Parking Along Water

Another sign says merely Keep Out. The only visual relief is a chain link fence decorated with flotsam from Casco Bay—gaily-colored lobster buoys.

As I say, in any other city the only residents of Union Wharf would be rats and the only visitors, muggers, rapists, and thieves. But this is Portland and among the several permanent human residents is an optimistic forty-ish woman named Karen Stimpson. Next to the boat on which she lives, occupying one of those steel-sided wharf buildings, is the headquarters of the Maine Island Trail Association (MITA).

Karen Stimpson calls her home the "Union Wharf Yacht Club," which tells you something about the barometric pressure of her personality. Together with her three cats, Stimpson has lived aboard *Juniata* for eleven years. It is not as if she has not had adequate exposure to the sea. She spent three years in the Merchant Marine, during which Third Mate Stimpson was at sea for four hundred days.

Juniata was built in 1920. She is a plumb-stemmed motor yacht with a box-shaped cabin and a wide swath of mahogany planking the length of her topsides. Built in the era when yacht was spelled with a capital *Y,* she has a unique bow cockpit for guests to sit in and "take the air" while someone else worries about soundings and ledges and ports of call. The cockpit resembles the rumble seat of an old-fashioned touring car except that it is in the front instead of the rear. The original owner used *Juniata* to take his friends on hunting trips; one frequent guest, L.L. Bean, declared that she was his "favorite boat."

I called Karen Stimpson because she is the official "Trail Keeper" of the Maine Island Trail Association, a division of the Island Institute. She promptly invited me for breakfast.

"I made a vow to myself," she explained after telling me of her experiences in the Merchant Marine and her years as a graphic designer (first for *Sail* magazine and then free-lance), "that at one point in my life I would take two years off and work for a conservation organization." The Maine Island Trail is a 325-mile long waterway, a necklace of sixty-five islands, stretching from Casco Bay all the way to Machias Bay, east of Schoodic Point. It is designed for the small boat—power, sail, canoe, or kayak—to wriggle along the coast and, with permission, use a collection of state-owned and private islands for low-impact recreation. The Association was formed to develop and maintain this nautical "trail."

The genius of the scheme is that it appeals to landowners and land-users alike. If you own an island in Maine and are not a full-time resident (the situation in the vast majority of the cases), there is little you can do to prevent trespassing, vandalism, the possibility of a devastating fire. We had seen generous, well-meaning property owners who have to rely on appeals to the public in the form of a sign nailed to a tree. But by joining MITA, the owner joins twenty-two hundred other members who have pledged not only to protect and care for the island but to *monitor* its use, too. It's like having thousands of guardian angels. As Karen Stimpson says, "It's an infectious idea."

Over the din of the squabbling Union Wharf gulls she continued, "After being involved for a short time, I started to open my eyes to the problems landowners have with public access. I could see both sides of the fence. For me, the idea that someone would pay a huge price for a piece of property and enormous taxes every year and be willing to share it was an extraordinary notion. And if I, a small-boat owner, was allowed to share it by assuming responsibility for it, then I would certainly rise to the occasion with great enthusiasm. It is very appealing to people who have been using islands or who want to use islands that *I am welcome on this island if I take care of it.*"

Karen Stimpson of the Maine Island Trail Association.

Members of the Adopt-an-Island Program have an even greater responsibility. They agree to assume the role of steward of a particular island, promising to visit at least once a month (more often, if possible), help keep it cleaned up, and monitor its use. Over and over again MITA has found that if islands are kept immaculate they remain that way for long periods. It is a phenomenon similar to that of the urban graffiti artist who gravitates to an already-marred wall; people who litter follow a herd instinct. Some unknown law of the human condition says that it is a lot harder to be the first one to litter. The Maine Island Trail Association seeks to capitalize on that simple precept.

"I've never felt so certain about anything," Stimpson said. "I have been watching both sides of this, and I am seeing a unique mix of generosity and conscientiousness. Generosity from the landowners, conscientiousness from everyone else. And, besides the excitement of seeing it work, you couldn't ask for a more enlightening or optimistic place to sit!"

Betsy and I were so taken with this unusual woman that we invited her to stay with us should she ever find herself in New York City. "That would be terrific," Karen Stimpson answered quick as a wink. "I'm really an easy guest. I don't even need a bed. All you have to do is set a plank between two rocking chairs, and I'm happy."

Early the next morning we resumed the pursuit of our own westbound trail—once again setting sail in the general direction of Kittery and the New Hampshire border.

Prouts Neck, an exclusive summer community, dangles like a small teat from the underbelly of Cape Elizabeth. We headed for this posh enclave on Saco Bay on a specific mission. Surrounded as it is by two of Maine's most touristical beaches, Scarborough and Old Orchard, Prouts Neck is in an unlikely spot for so private a settlement. But *private* it is. So much so that we had a devil of a time finding the only public part of it—Winslow Homer's studio.

For the last twenty-five years of his life until he died in 1910, Homer lived there and painted some of the masterpieces for which he is world famous. If, as you sail around Cape Elizabeth, you think that the area looks familiar, it is. You have seen it before—on the walls of the National Gallery and the Boston Museum of Fine Arts and the Philadelphia Museum of Art and the Cleveland Museum and the Metropolitan Museum of Art.

To my photographer's eye, you simply cannot find a painter who masters objective reality better than Winslow Homer. *The Fog Warning, The Herring Net* (both 1885), and everyone's favorite, *Eight Bells* (1886), to name a few, movingly capture the drama, cruelty, and sense of impending danger of life at sea unlike the work of any other artist. For someone like me who has also tried to preserve the aura of a mid-ocean gale, I have to marvel at Homer's stirring portraits of nature's wrath.

You would have thought that we were trying to find out the location of a local movie star's house and that the residents were trying to protect their famous neighbor's privacy, so reticent was *anybody* to tell me where Homer's studio was. It is, after all, a National Historic Landmark. A walk through Prouts Neck is a little like playing dodge 'em with No Trespassing signs. The signs are, to put it mildly, ubiquitous. After making several attempts to ask directions of children who were bicycling to their tennis lessons, I gave up. Did I look like a child molester? I wondered. I stopped in at the tony Black Point Inn (jackets and ties only, please) and asked a steward where the Winslow Homer Studio was. Now I'm not going to call this man a liar, but when he told me that he was new and didn't know *exactly* how to direct me there I began to get very paranoid feelings. Do summer resorts hire their help in August? Had I stinted on the Right Guard? Did I need both a candy mint *and* a breath mint?

Eventually, sharp-eyed Eliza spotted a discreet sign. It was flanked by two others that said, respectively, Only Way Out This Way and No Parking at Any Time. The smallest of the three signs indicated the path to the studio. We'd made it. *Phew!*

It was worth the trouble to stand alone in this wonderfully under-curated museum. It is family run and sits next to a house in which Homer's grandnephew, Charles Homer Willauer, still lives. No one was there when we were, and it smelled suitably mildewy. The walls are covered with bad reproductions of Homer paintings, and in the center of the room is a large dining table. Surrounded by six straight backed chairs with worn beige upholstery, the table is littered with books and magazine articles about the artist. There is no phony easel set up with a "half-finished painting." All you get is the musty atmosphere of another era and the ghost of a genius.

I kept a promise to Eliza that we would visit the amusement park at nearby Old Orchard Beach. She had spent enough time on the boat—poor only-child that she is—to deserve a kid's outing. She was gratifyingly excited, and I tried not to let on how tickled I was at the prospect of competing for a Kewpie doll.

Old Orchard Beach is truly another Maine. I had to keep reminding myself that I was only three and one-half miles from and in full view of Prouts Neck's tennis courts. The beach itself is one of the widest and longest in Maine. Coney Island on the Fourth of July or Venice Beach year-round could not boast more half-naked bodies per square inch than we saw broiling themselves on Old Orchard Beach that afternoon. A tourist destination for French Canadians (the appropriate exit off the Maine Turnpike is, I am told, marked *Sortie 5*), the beach is thoroughly bilingual.

Heading straight for the rides, we resisted come-ons for "French Fries/ Pommes Frites," "99¢ Sunglasses," "The Bona Vista Motel," and the "Louie, Louie Restaurant and Lounge." The first ride, the SuperStar was bad. The YoYo was worse. And the Pirate was the worst of all. Eliza loved all three, although she admitted that the Pirate was "sickitating." The Pirate ride is a double-ended boat, which as many as twenty-seven people can sit in, suspended from an axle at the top of an enormous four-legged stanchion. It was painted a revolting shade of yellow. It didn't much resemble a pirate ship although there was a forecastle at one end, a sterncastle at the other, and a mast-like object in the middle. The seats at either end face toward the center. The Pirate swings pendulum-like through an arc of 180 degrees.

In the worst weather imaginable *Consolation* could never make you as nauseated as the Pirate does. Eliza and I sat at one end of the "ship" and a young mother, whose sleeveless arms were covered with tattoos, sat with her son at the other. There were no other riders. About halfway through the ride the boy we were facing began to look queasy. You know when a swing pauses at the top of its arc and seems to hover there for a fraction of a second? It was at this precise moment when we were looking directly up at them that the boy wailed, "Mom, I gotta get off. I'm gonna puke!"

Eliza and I looked at one another in horror. What could we do but pray? Miraculously, the moment passed, the pendulum returned, and it was not until we were looking *down* on them that the boy let go.

Old Orchard Beach: Eliza and I eschewed *pommes frites* in favor of a ride called The Pirate.

The afternoon was warm to the point of being soporific. We were off the wind sailing over a gentle offshore swell. We passed Biddeford Pool on our starboard beam.

It was with great sadness that I began to think that our trip would soon end. I had reached that point in a long voyage when one can't really imagine life *off* the boat. One gets so accustomed to the rhythm of the sea, the tides, the early nights and early mornings, the freedom to go or stay as one pleases. But it was too soon for such thoughts.

The plan was to continue to Kittery, thus completing our self-assigned voyage. But afterwards we would double back and take leave of *Consolation* at the Portland Yacht Club in Falmouth Foreside. Fred and Joyce Crane had plans for some nautical leaf-peeping during Maine's early autumn. And on the way back we would spend a night in Biddeford Pool, where an aunt of Betsy's lives.

We sailed toward Kennebunkport. The wind was out of the west and Dicken with an impish grin suggested we continue sailing right into the Kennebunk River. It was the kind of wise-guy stunt I love Dicken for—something on the order of the pilot who insists on flying *under* bridges. The channel between the two breakwaters is only fifty feet wide, and there was a lot of sunny Saturday afternoon traffic. We screamed in, dodging motor boats, mainsail and full genoa jib flying, past Gooch's Beach and the Colony Hotel, past Government Wharf, past the Nonantum Hotel, all the way up to the Arundel Yacht Club in the heart of busy, downtown Kennebunkport. It was exhilarating and stupid. But we made it safely. I don't think I will ever be photographed so many times the rest of my life as I was that day!

Rusticators aside, what we had seen in the course of our travels this summer was a Maine full of people who had much to be concerned about. These were tough economic times. But, incredibly, the image of the Mainer as the rugged individualist, survivor, and master of his own destiny is no mere myth.

Two thoroughly modern incarnations of this Yankee legacy are entrepreneurs, Tom and Kate Chappell. In Kennebunk I made a point of calling on the two cofounders of the nation's top-selling natural personal care products company, Tom's of Maine.

Launched with a five-thousand dollar loan from a friend, Tom's of Maine produced Clearlake, the first liquid nonphosphate laundry detergent in 1970. In a matter of weeks the Kennebunk post office was overrun with empty Clearlake bottles, which were returned postpaid for refill.

We sat in the Chappells' spacious garden behind their house on Kennebunk's main street. We munched on delicious sandwiches (yes, mine did have bean sprouts) while we talked.

The company's current products, over two decades later, include Tom's Natural Mouthwash, Tom's Natural Deodorant, Tom's Natural Flossing Ribbon, and Tom's Natural Toothpaste. Ingredients like coriander, propolis, and myrrh are squeezed into recyclable packaging, which always has a cute message (printed in soy-based ink) from "Your friends, Tom and Kate." But there is nothing cute about the $16 million in sales this Mom and Pop company had last year and there

Saco Bay: The *Shelly Ann* is loaded high with a fresh string of traps.

is utter seriousness about the corporate philosophy of Tom's of Maine. Tom and Kate's "friends" used to be the customers of the local natural food store. Now they are the customers of the 760-outlet CVS chain as well as buyers in England, Taiwan, and Singapore. When United States Marines burst into the home of General Manuel Noriega during the 1989 American invasion of Panama, they found Tom's Natural Toothpaste in the medicine cabinet.

"I have made the transition," said Chappell, "from a 'rugged individualist' benefiting from the heritage and traditions of the free enterprise system to someone who said, if I'm going to be in business I'm going to be responsible and ethical—and shrewd."

If we had any doubt that these two were not everyday, run-of-the-mill business executives, we learned otherwise. Kate Chappell is an accomplished, widely-shown watercolorist of Maine landscapes. Tom recently received a Master's of Theology Degree from the Harvard Divinity School. Twice weekly for two years he drove the two hours from Kennebunk to Cambridge to mull over issues of ethics and morality in business. Out of his divinity school experience, and nine months of dialogue among Tom, Kate, and everyone else at Tom's—from the directors to the assemblers on the production line—a Mission Statement emerged.

"Now the Mission Statement is the thing that drives our business," Chappell said. "It is the value system, the vision, that is qualitative not quantitative." Sound like a lot of liberal hogwash? Well, the truth is it works. Is it possible to do well by doing good? Absolutely. And you can measure their success by either of two yardsticks (depending on your bias), by the fact that they never lost sight of their founding principles or by that good old American yardstick, the profit and loss

The Long Beach at York: One of the broad sand beaches found only on the western coast.

statement: Tom and Kate have sold a lot of toothpaste.

The next morning, feeling perhaps more introspective after our visit with the Chappells, we set sail for the homestretch. There was a steady westerly, and *Consolation* showed her customary verve slicing through the waves close to the wind. The mood on board was quiet. No one seemed to feel that it was a day for chatter. Eliza stayed below and worked on a painting. Betsy sat by herself on the foredeck, reading. There is a nice spot to lean against the forward bulkhead of the trunk cabin, and, if you bring a pillow from the cockpit, it becomes a cozy spot to read and be by yourself. Dicken gave me company aft while he practiced playing his guitar. I steered toward Kittery.

In what seemed like no time we found ourselves at the mouth of Portsmouth Harbor. I did something I can't always do: I forced a change in my mood. We had after all made it; we'd sailed the coast of Maine from stem to stern. And what a summer we'd had!

"Kittery at last!!!" I called out, pretending to be Admiral Peary at the Pole. Well, maybe Lieutenant (j.g.) Peary would be more fitting, but at least I rallied the

Kittery at last!!!

crew. Betsy came aft, Eliza came above, and Dicken laughed.

If my memory serves me, I think we opened that last bottle of wine.

The final disembarkation is always a melancholy affair, but it would still be another day or two before we planned to anchor *Consolation* for the last time at the Portland Yacht Club.

No, instead it was with a sense of elation and accomplishment that I called out, "Ready about. *Hard alee!*" I spun *Consolation*'s wheel hard over. Dicken tailed the genoa sheet while Betsy winched it in. We tacked in front of a U.S. Navy submarine docked at the Portsmouth Navy Yard, and, leaving Kittery astern, we sailed smartly out of Portsmouth Harbor, making for Biddeford Pool.

Eighteen

A LITTLE BOAT LOOKING FOR A HARBOR

One of my most vivid early childhood memories was awakening in the predawn darkness of August 30, 1954, to the raging seas and winds that was Hurricane Carol. Those childhood memories came back to me when, as we sat on a guest mooring in Biddeford Pool, we first learned that a hurricane with the business-like name *Bob* was threatening Cape Hatteras.

We were seated below around the all-purpose saloon table having a Sunday morning cup of coffee before going ashore for a breakfast visit with Betsy's Aunt Joan. It was a gray, drizzly morning, dank, windy, and chilly. We were a little over halfway between Kittery and the Portland Yacht Club. Eliza, snuggled in my sleeping bag in the forward cabin, wrote to her school friends on her seemingly inexhaustible supply of puffin postcards. She was contentedly unaware that our snug little home away from home might soon be in jeopardy. The radio was tuned to NOAA (National Oceanic and Atmospheric Administration) radio, which broadcasts the weather forecasts on which mariners rely. I looked at my watch, saw it was time for an update, and shushed everyone up. We listened carefully. "This is the voice of the National Weather Service in Portland, Maine," said an announcer in a no-nonsense tone of voice. "Broadcasting over NOAA Radio. Good Morning."

He continued: "The following is an advisory issued by the National Hurricane Center: Although it is too early to tell where, when, or even if northern New England will be directly affected by Hurricane Bob, latest computer and satellite guidance suggest that Northern New England's weather may be significantly influenced by Hurricane Bob. Be advised: This is a very dangerous storm. Hurricane Bob is presently packing winds of one hundred miles per hour."

I heard a collective "oh shit." Dicken, always the optimist though, broke the silence with some reassuring thoughts. Bob was still a good eight hundred miles away, we were moored in a reasonably well protected anchorage, and we were all hungry, so why not go to Joan Kittredge's for breakfast. With no further urging we climbed into *Hoggie* and rowed to the Biddeford Pool Yacht Club float.

Biddeford Pool is a only three miles from the glitz and sleaze of Old Orchard Beach, but it might as well be light years away. The Pool itself is a large tidal inlet, which seems spacious at high tide. Crowded together is a mixture of pleasure craft and working boats. The small anchorage is encircled by marsh grass at low water, and you can see why the boats are moored so close together. A narrow channel shaped like the neck of a bottle and known as The Gut separates The Pool from the Gulf of Maine and insulates it from almost everything but the rushing waters of the flood and ebb of the tides.

Breakfast was sensational. For some reason that particular morning, the hot coffee and toasted bagels tasted better in her warm, dry, motionless kitchen than they would have below decks on *Consolation.* I think we were all grateful. It was fun to see Joan and her daughter, Martha, again. Indeed, for a few bacon-and-egg-filled moments, Hurricane Bob seemed unimportant.

Pretty soon, though, the gusty wind rattling the windowpanes shook me out of my brief placation. The threatening storm reclaimed my attention. I suggested we call Fred Crane at home in Dalton. As owner of *Consolation,* Fred, Dicken and I agreed, should make the potentially critical decision: Namely, where *Consolation* should ride out the storm, if Bob did indeed get to Maine.

When I reached him by phone from Joan's kitchen, I explained where we were and that *Consolation* was on a secure mooring in one of the less crowded parts of the anchorage. Fred listened carefully and after a moment said that, while Biddeford Pool was not the ideal harbor in which to ride out a hurricane, it was better than most.

"Yeah, come to think of it," he decided, "why don't you just stay right where you are." Fred paused again and then added, "Remember one thing, though: Boats are replaceable and you guys aren't. Don't take any unnecessary chances." I assured Fred we would not and would be in touch. We hung up.

I turned to Joan, summer resident of Biddeford Pool for many years. "Who," I asked, "would be the person to see about staying in The Pool?"

It is times like these when one is thankful for any local contact to turn to for assistance. But having a local *relative* felt like an unanticipated bonus. Joan telephoned Marshall Alexander, who just happened to be Biddeford Pool's harbormaster, a lobsterman, *and* Joan's old friend. "I don't know anyone who knows the sea better than Marshall . . . or who has more informed local knowledge," she told us after a brief conversation. "He said he'd wait for you down at the fish pier."

We hastened back to the harbor. Marshall Alexander was waiting just where he had said he would be. A stocky man, Alexander had the rough hands and weather-worn face of a veteran fisherman. He seemed to have a straightforward air about him. In that regard, he did not disappoint us. Without anything further than a quick hello, Marshall Alexander said, "Have some bad news for you folks. 'Fraid you can't stay here."

I think it would be fair to interject here that anyone who knows us, if asked for a thumbnail personality sketch, would not think to use the words "taciturn" or "laconic" or "incommunicative" to describe any of us. At that moment, however, we were collectively struck dumb.

Mr. Alexander, as I now mentally called him, explained in his matter-of-fact manner that the owners of the moorings in The Pool, members of the Biddeford Pool Yacht Club, were, as he spoke, racing back to reclaim them. There would not be enough moorings to go around when everyone returned. He further explained his rationale for denying us a mooring by saying that we had ample time to find another harbor. When Hurricane Bob got closer, he said, there would be boats arriving on an emergency, last-minute basis, and he would not be able to turn them away. Lastly, he told us in a confidential, just-between-us tone of voice, "The Pool's not such a great place to be in a hurricane anyway. Too crowded. Too exposed to the northeast." If he meant this to cheer us up, he was unsuccessful.

In retrospect I bear Alexander no ill will. His friends and neighbors were his first responsibility; nobody would begrudge him that. He was not wrong on his second point either; we did have time to search elsewhere. However well-intentioned, though, Alexander had dealt us an unexpected joker, a disheartening one at that.

Joan had tried her best, too, and we were all grateful for her efforts. But suddenly it was palpably time to go. In the steady drizzle, we said unenthusiastic good-byes. We thanked Joan for breakfast and for her pains. I realized we had more to do and think about than we had a few minutes earlier, and I was anxious to get underway. I thought unhappily of Arthur Miller's characterization of Willy Loman: "a little boat looking for a harbor."

Dicken steered *Consolation* out of The Pool under power. There was a strong incoming tide as he negotiated the Gut. We bisected the channel between Stage Island and Negro Island, passed the red and white bell buoy, and ran right smack into a dense offshore fog bank.

The fog was thick—not thick enough to qualify as thick o' fog and surely not in the dungeon thick o' fog category—but visibility was reduced to the extent that we felt it would be prudent to plot a course from buoy to buoy as we groped our way down east. It helped to tick the buoys off one by one as we progressed and thus keep a reasonably reassuring notion of where we were.

We were sailing without a destination, which is never particularly agreeable when you know you have to get somewhere, and Bob, NOAA radio informed us, was growing more ferocious by the hour. With Betsy at the helm, her eyes sharp on the compass and straining to see ahead into the fog, we sailed an almost-too-rapid broad reach up the coast and were discomforted, too, by the batteries of heavy southerly swells rolling underneath us.

Dicken and I went below to consult *Consolation*'s ship's library. We needed to do a lot of hurricane homework fast.

Mission number one was to find a "hurricane hole." I was not exactly sure what defined a hurricane hole since I had never had occasion to look for one. To me it was one of those romantic, faraway destinations—the stuff of Nordhoff and Hall or Robert Louis Stevenson—that all people who sail know of and bandy about but never actually need. Well, we needed one now, but we did not actually *know* of one.

I have praised the cruising guide Hank and Jan Taft wrote before. I thought of them as friends sailing along with us, giving us the benefit of their considerable experience cruising Maine's coast. Although I did not know him, I had lamented

Hank's untimely death in 1991 as I might an old shipmate's. It was thus to the Taft's book that we turned first. We researched Taft as well as Duncan and Ware's venerable cruising guide and Alfred Loomis's *Ranging the Maine Coast.* After studying as many relevant sections as we could, Dicken and I warmed to a harbor called The Basin. Its many advantages seemed to outweigh its sole disadvantage: it was still thirty-five miles away, and it would take at least six hours to get there.

In an increasingly boisterous sea, we agonized over each of the many places the books recommended, but we kept returning to our first bet. The Basin is a completely landlocked sanctuary protected by a narrow S-shaped entrance; it is situated across the New Meadows River from the unpretentious working harbor of Cundys, well west of The Basin where Betsy and I had sat on a rock—it seemed like eons ago—remembering her father. Dicken and I pored over the chart, reread the books, but it was the description written by the Tafts that convinced us that it was to The Basin we must hurry: "Here is what many yachtsmen dream about when they ponder the ultimate safe harbor: a small lake surrounded by rocky points and dark green trees, with hardly a sign of human habitation, completely protected from every direction, and the water still as a millpond. . . . For this part of the world this is the best site for a hurricane hole."

We made our decision, and I think we all felt better for it. We would sail toward The Basin as quickly as the fog would safely permit, and we would hope our haven-to-be would prove as meritorious as advertised. Dicken went up into the cockpit to spell Betsy, and I continued to research hurricane-related topics in the aforementioned books as well as old standbys like *Eldridge Tide and Pilot* and *Reed's Nautical Almanac and Coast Pilot*—reference books no skipper should sail without.

Hurricanes, it turns out, rarely get as far north as the coast of Maine. There have, however, been some dramatic exceptions: notably an unannounced hurricane in September 1938, which killed six hundred people. Striking in an era when tropical depressions were neither tracked nor given personifying names (female *or* male), the Hurricane of 1938, as it came to be called, proved devastating for all of New England. As it headed toward Maine, it caused massive destruction. En route the hurricane's eye passed over my old childhood haunt, Fenwick. The storm destroyed most of Fenwick's fleet of Indian-class racing sloops. Our house in those days had had a deeply shading front porch on the side facing Long Island Sound. The hurricane tore it right off, and sadly it was never restored. It was the storm surge—that is the rise in sea level caused by a major cyclonic depression—rather than the wind that destroyed our porch. Fifteen miles down the shore in New London the same surge left an ocean-going freighter on top of the Thames River bridge.

In my research, I learned that a hurricane, a cyclone, and a typhoon are all the same, that is, they are all cyclonic atmospheric disturbances characterized by masses of air rapidly rotating around a low-pressure center. In the northern hemisphere they rotate counter-clockwise, and in the southern, clockwise. Only their location determines their name: Typhoons are spawned west of the International

Date Line, hurricanes east of it, and cyclones form in the Indian Ocean.

Another item I learned is really only useful if you happen to find yourself in the middle of a hurricane, but in that unhappy event it truly can be useful. What you do is stand facing into the full force of the hurricane's wind (kids, don't try this at home), spread your arms in the crucifixion position, and bend them back as far as is comfortable. Your right arm will be pointing at the eye of the hurricane. Seriously.

In the fifty-plus years since 1938 only five hurricanes, I learned, have advanced up the eastern seaboard as far as Maine. There were two in 1954: the double whammy of Carol and her nearly-as-infamous stepsister, Edna, a storm that all but obliterated the racing fleet of the Portland Yacht Club. Donna made it in 1960, Ginny in 1963, and Hurricane Gloria, the winds of which exceeded 130 miles per hour, in 1985.

As we mulled over all this aboard *Consolation,* it seemed to us that the odds were in our favor. First, hurricanes rarely get to Maine. Second, when they do, they almost invariably do so in September. It had been thirty-seven Augusts since the last hurricane had clobbered the coast of Maine in August. (And that, by the way, was my old friend Hurricane Carol.)

So, we resolved to head for The Basin until we received news to suggest otherwise. If Hurricane Bob veered out to sea, our only failing would have been adding an unnecessary thirty-five miles to *Consolation*'s log. We concurred that under the circumstances that would be no great sacrifice. But I also resolved not to forget the timeless advice of Duncan and Ware: "The presence of a hurricane off Puerto Rico, Florida, or even Carolina need give the [Maine] skipper no cause for alarm. . . . But if the lady reaches New Jersey, it is well to seek a landlocked anchorage and look to one's ground tackle."

It was a great relief when, at last, we wriggled through the S-shaped entrance to The Basin. As the gray skies became dusky, we found a spot to drop the hook a little to the north of the permanent anchorage. There were only eight or ten boats moored there, leaving enough swinging room for a whole fleet of sailboats. In a hurricane, just as high seas are more dangerous to a moored boat than high winds, a crowded harbor of boats dragging their anchors and fouling one another is potentially catastrophic compared to a lone boat dragging ashore.

We felt quite snug and optimistic for the first time in twenty-four hours, and although the chilly drizzle persisted we found comradely warmth below decks. I chipped a few cube-sized chunks of ice, dropped them in glasses, and mixed drinks. We joined in a toast to Betsy for finding The Basin after thirty-five miles of fog. Gesturing to my still-raised glass, I added with dark humor, "I hope nothing except one of these will be "on the rocks" tomorrow night." Nine-year-old Eliza looked a little perplexed, but when I kissed her good night a few minutes later she seemed to be the only one among us who would sleep soundly that night.

We arose early, knowing we had much to do. After coffee and a quick bowl of cereal, Dicken and I donned foul weather gear—the rain had been steady all night and was continuing—as we waited for NOAA's 6:00 A.M. bulletin. Through our friends, the operators at Camden Marine, we made calls to Fred Crane to let him know where we were and to Coe Kittredge, who generously volunteered to drive up from Boston to help out.

NOAA informed that the chance of Bob striking the coast of Maine had been upgraded from a Hurricane Watch to a Hurricane Warning: "A hurricane warning means hurricane force winds of 74 miles an hour or higher can be expected. This is a very dangerous storm packing maximum sustained winds of 115 miles per hour. The storm is accelerating to the northeast at 35 miles per hour. This means that the eye of the hurricane should reach and move along the southern Maine coastline between five and eight this evening. Mariners, be aware that seas will gradually build to 20 to 30 feet by this evening with sustained winds between 60 and 100 knots. Residents of southern Maine should rush to complete prestorm preparations over the next hour or so as very little time remains before the onset of the hurricane force winds."

We took this last bit of advice seriously.

Our first priority was to anchor ourselves as securely as possible. But how? Just

Dicken brings Coe aboard as we prepare for Hurricane Bob. At Coe's feet is the coil of heater hose we would use to prevent the anchor lines from chafing through at the chocks.

before we had left Biddeford Pool, we had met a fisherman with a strong Scandinavian accent. He'd lived in the Caribbean for a number of years on board a sailboat and described for us the so-called Bahamian Rig, a system of anchoring about which none of us had ever heard. The theory is that if you set your primary anchor (biggest or best or both) to windward of where you expect the storm to hit and your secondary anchor 180 degrees away from the first and attach both anchor lines with as much scope (length) as you have aboard to the bow, you will have two very important advantages over other anchoring systems. First, if anchor one fails, you have a backup. No one can deny the obvious benefit of that, but perhaps a more important feature of the Bahamian Rig is the fact that your boat will only swing about its own length, making it much less likely that you will foul other boats in a crowded harbor.

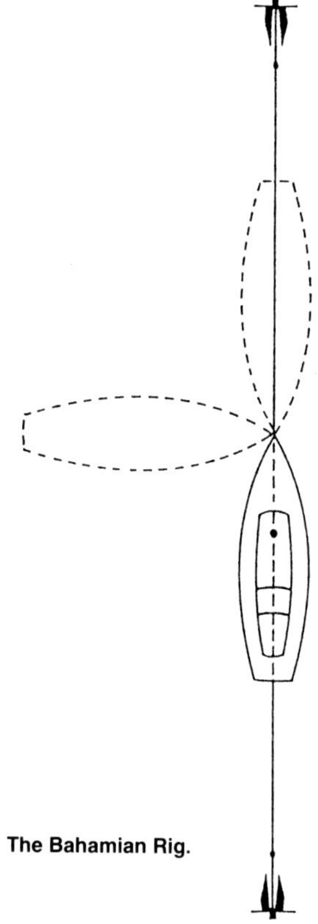

The Bahamian Rig.

In heavy rain we went about setting the two anchors, using *Consolation*'s engine to drop the big Danforth and *Hoggie* to place the smaller one in the opposite direction. At one point Betsy stuck her head up the companionway and said, ominously, "The barometer's starting to drop. Really drop." With that, she disappeared back below. (In the end we would learn from the newspapers that Bob's minimum central pressure—29.09 inches—was the lowest ever recorded in Maine in August.)

Four waterborne visitors stopped by. the first was a friendly guy from a nearby sailboat. We gossiped about this and that—anchors, the supposed virtues of The Basin, the direction from which we expected the winds. As we talked we watched more and more boats streaming into The Basin. After a spell he rowed off into the rain. Lucky we were not superstitious; his skiff was named the *Enola Gay,* after the plane which dropped the atomic bomb onto Hiroshima.

In the end we would learn from the newspapers that Bob's minimum central pressure—29.09 inches—was the lowest ever recorded in Maine in August.

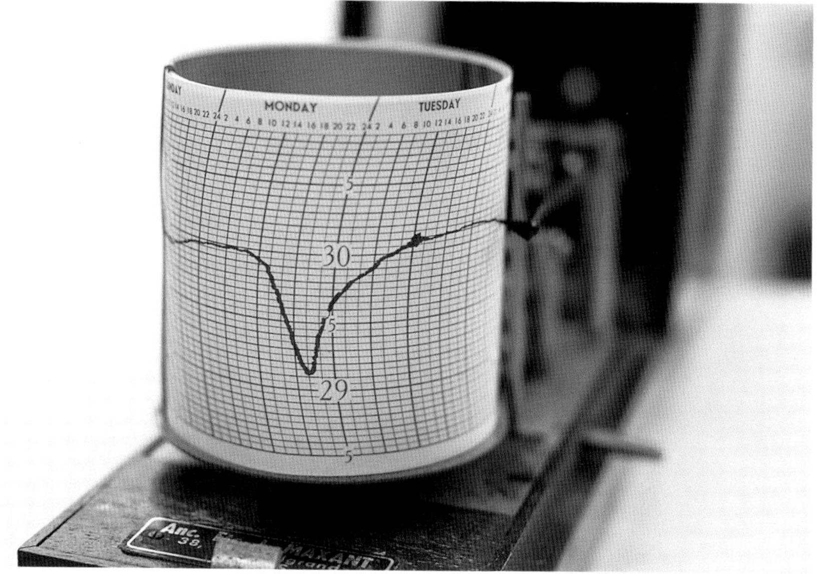

The second pair of visitors were two smiling older women—an unlikely pair given the conditions—cosseted in orange slickers with hoods tightly tied, piloting a dinghy with a small outboard motor. They asked if we were planning to remain aboard during the storm. This was a question that had obviously occurred to each of us, but one which we had, I suppose, unconsciously avoided discussing. I replied honestly that I was not sure. "See that white house up on the hill?" one of them said, pointing ashore. "That's our house. You are all welcome to spend the night with us. The door is open." On that incredibly decent note they gave us a wave and powered off. We watched them stop one by one at every boat in the harbor—there were now at least forty—tendering the same invitation.

The third visitor was none other than Coe himself who had raced up from Boston to lend a hand.

Setting the Bahamian Rig. We hoped it would save *Consolation*—and us.

As the barometer continued to fall, Coe, Dicken, and I rigged chafing gear where the anchor line could wear through (Coe had brought heater hose for this purpose), lashed the mainsail securely to the boom, and removed the huge roller-reefed genoa. We had to winch Dicken up in the bo'sun's chair to accomplish this last task. When we felt generally shipshape and storm-rigged, we repaired below for a meeting to discuss the plans, which so much busy work had seduced us into postponing.

To stay aboard or seek safety ashore is a perennial dilemma for cruising mariners facing a serious blow. I had without speaking about it with Betsy arrived at the decision that Betsy and Eliza should avail themselves of the extraordinary generosity of the two sisters in the outboard, Mary and Eleanor, and suffer the storm on land. This may sound old-fashioned (or in the lexicon of today, *sexist*), a little too much of "women and children first" for some tastes. But I believed two things: It would be irresponsible to put a nine-year-old unnecessarily in harm's way, and someone had to be with her during the storm. We drank some cold coffee, and I broached the subject. To my surprise, Betsy said fine, I agree. I think I actually detected a faint hint of relief.

The unspoken upshot of our meeting was that Dicken, Coe, and I would remain aboard *Consolation.*

By midafternoon the weather was getting really, well, shitty. We began the nervous-making wait for the full force of the hurricane, relieved only by the fact that Betsy and Eliza were now safely in the sisters' farmhouse. I transferred some of my frustration onto NOAA; they consistently broadcast the storm's position hours late. At 3:27 P.M., for example, they reported the location of Bob as of 11:15 A.M.—more than four hours late. Weather may be difficult to predict, but NOAA has the ability to track the eye of a hurricane inch by inch. If you are anticipating a major storm, you want to know exactly where it is every minute because from that information you can easily extrapolate when you will be visited. I did bless NOAA, however, for unintentional humor. At the end of each update we would hear: Now for the mid-coastal hay advisory. Drying conditions will not be good today.

In fact, we received more up-to-date information from a commercial station in Boston, WBZ. They were terrific about keeping us informed of Bob's location. We did pay for the privilege, however. Interspersed between hurricane bulletins were songs like Bob Dylan's "Shelter from the Storm," the Doors' "Riders on the Storm," and, of course, "You Are Like a Hurricane" by Neil Young.

While we waited, Dicken caught up on his entries in the ship's log, and Coe and I mostly fidgeted. Every once in a while we would tune to the VHF chatter among the fishermen. Through the saloon porthole in the heavy rain I could see many boats by this time: a large dragger called the *Julie D.* out of nearby Cundys Harbor, an old sardiner, and many lobster boats rafting together two or three abreast. Working boats still streamed into The Basin even at this late date. It was encouraging to see them; it gave us confidence that we were in the right place.

Almost all the radio conversations were between wives and their husbands. In these, the message was always the same: "Leave your damn boat and come home!" Sure enough, at about four o'clock, when we were just beginning to see whitecaps

The brunt of Bob dropped an inch of rain an hour—eight inches before the depression left us.

in The Basin, Betsy called on the walkie-talkie. She reported that one of the men seeking refuge at the sisters' house said we should expect severe tornadoes on top of the hurricane. He added that we were "dumb" to stay aboard. I told Betsy that I would radio her back.

Finally, the time had come for the fellows to explain exactly why we *were* staying aboard. Not just to Betsy but to ourselves. Was it macho foolishness or would our nautical skills, such as they were, mean the difference between saving and losing our beloved *Consolation*? At the very least we owed ourselves a rational analysis of the risks we faced. Of the three of us, I was the only one married with a child; Dicken was in the final stages of a divorce, but to complicate matters was expecting a child with his girlfriend Tobie; and Coe had neither wife nor child to stir into the mix. Not to be melodramatic, we also had our own lives to consider.

Dicken, our own Billy Budd, saw situations like the one we faced in very simple terms: He was unafraid and, I believe, never really thought twice about leaving the ship. Coe and I grappled more openly with the decision—and with our own apprehension. I noticed Coe's consumption of Camel Lights was on the rise, and, although maneuvering space in *Consolation*'s saloon was limited, I managed my pacing as well as any lion in a cage. Dicken calmly diverted himself by catching up on his entries in the ship's log while lending half an ear to the conversation. At one point Dicken interrupted our ruminations.

He said, plainspokenly, "Look, you guys can stay or go. I'm staying just because I know if anchors start dragging in here there will be something positive I know I'll be able to do. And three of us could probably do it better." There was no sense of coercion, but, like the Three Musketeers, we were at last all for one and one for all. Tacitly, the decision had been made. I radioed Betsy.

The time from the point when we decided to ride out the storm until the full force of the hurricane hit us passed swiftly. The brunt of Bob dropped an inch of rain an hour—eight inches before the depression left us. And the wind, she howled and screamed. Evergreens on the shore bent flat over under the onslaught. The cacophony of wind through tree and rigging alike was a fearsome dissonance. Through it all, though, The Basin sheltered us. Never were the seas given an opportunity to build into anything more than small whitecaps, nothing more serious than you would expect on a lake on a brisk autumn afternoon. The high winds roiled the rain and the spray off the sea was driven horizontally, but *Consolation* pulled firmly yet steadily on her anchor line, hardly either pitching or yawing. We could only imagine what it must have been like on the high seas outside the protecting bluffs and trees of our sanctuary.

Dicken and I went forward to gauge the strain on our main anchor and to check for signs of chaffing. Suddenly, very close to us through the swirl of sea and rain we saw a sailboat under power struggling against the wind, trying to re-anchor. Indeed this was our worst fear in the now crowded anchorage: that boats with 150 to 200 feet of anchor line out would start dragging and fouling one another. The boat was from Hingham, Massachusetts. A woman was at the helm and a man was on the foredeck wrestling with the anchoring gear. I could just make out the boat's name; she was called *Fore.* If you play golf, you will appreciate the double enten-

---

***Eagle Wing III* did not fare as well as we did.**

EAGLE WING III

dre of this ketch's name. In golf when your ball is about to hit someone, you shout *FORE!*

The couple on *Fore* seemed at their wit's end as they tried to find a spot clear of anyone else's lines. Eventually the husband dropped the hook (and many, many feet of chain) over the side directly on top of our anchor line. Up on *Consolation*'s bow, Dicken and I shouted at them against the howling wind, "You're fouling our anchor line! Get away from us!" Dicken dropped to his knees and put his hand on the rope. "Oh, Jesus," he yelled, "I can feel his chain [dragging across our anchor line]." I hollered as loudly as I could, and, in spite of myself, started cursing the hapless mariners-in-distress. It may seem selfish, but there was nothing we could do to help him, and there was a great deal he could do to hurt us. He had to disentangle himself from us or our anchor would drag and we would have to move, possibly causing a domino effect of boats careening around the crowded harbor. His wife, who was at the helm, at last acknowledged our shouts with a wave, and they were able to retrieve their anchor without bringing ours up with it. A little way off they maneuvered into a clear hole and successfully re-anchored.

Just as that little mess resolved itself, two sport-fishing boats, which were rafted side-by-side dragged *their* anchor and were swept toward us. Between them and us, however, were two lobster boats tied together fore and aft. The lobsterman on the forward of the two boats in jeopardy seemed awfully calm under the circumstances—a great deal calmer than we felt aboard the next boat in the path of this accident-about-to-happen. In fact, he shouted over to us, "We're in a fine mess now!" Three burly guys were on the bow of one of the sport-fishers straining to recover their anchor and in the process slipping and swearing and sliding on the rain-swept deck. When they were only a few feet from the first lobsterman, one of them pulled his knife and slashed at his own anchor line. When he severed it, it was so taut that the release sounded like a rifle shot. I shouted my thanks, but I am sure they did not hear me. As the sport-fishers powered away, I could see the name on the transom of the one that had had to cut its line. She was called *Misfit.*

In rapid fire succession another boat, a very large ketch (a good 60 feet) dragged anchor and, like a bumper car at a carnival, careened through The Basin completely out of control. Like *Fore* this ketch was undermanned for the situation. The bowman did not have the strength to cope with the heavy gear; his shipmate, who was so far aft as to be out of earshot, had to power through a maze to avoid wrecking other boats. We watched in horror as did all the other manned boats in The Basin. In the end, we witnessed an example of consummate seamanship, which seemed extraordinary, but which, I realized, is completely fundamental to the ethos of the Maine seafarer. The crew of the big dragger, the *Julie D.*, dispatched its skiff with two very able seamen. They motored to where the ketch was floundering, boarded her, and helped get her over to the *Julie D.*'s mooring. The captain of the *Julie D.* gave his precious mooring to the ketch and—to the silent cheers of all who watched—powered out of The Basin to weather the remainder of Hurricane Bob on the high seas.

By eight o'clock the 60 knot winds were replaced with the eerie calm of the eye of the storm. (NOAA later reported that the precise center of the storm at

8:00 P.M. was at 43.5°N and 69.9°W, which I plotted to be two miles from The Basin.) The aftermath of the passing of the eye was not as severe (although it often can be worse). The bulk of the storm system passed to our east; we had experienced the west (less brutal) sector of the hurricane.

And then it was over. The rain continued, the wind still whistled, but we knew with absolute certainty that we were safe. We had made it.

Morning dawned clearly and crisply. It was a perfect fall day, bright and clear with a deeply polarized, almost navy blue sky. Hurricane Bob was, for those of us

Magadisen* was the big ketch rescued by the *Julie D.

YAMAHA

who had escaped harm, yesterday's memory. After coffee we jumped into *Hoggie* and rowed over to the big ketch.

They told us how scared they had been, how their anchor had been fouled on a lobster pot the whole time although they had not known it. They told us of their rescue by the noble crew of the *Julie D.* and finally what the captain had said when they tried to thank him.

"It's nothing. . . . Maybe you'll be able to help me out someday."

EPILOGUE

LUCK HAD PERCHED on our spars all summer. Sure, we had occasionally fired up the Iron Main, but most of the time we had enjoyed abundant winds and fair tides. The extent of our cruising was limited only by the gentle pace a sailboat so delightfully imposes. We had had, by all accounts, the most fog-free summer in living memory. Maine mulls can paralyze cruising yachtsmen—and lobstermen, too—for weeks on end. For us, the fog wisped in as an infrequent, welcome diversion. More often than not we had the luxury of reveling in its eerie beauty rather than fearing the hazards it concealed.

We had survived Hurricane Bob. And the rest of the time we had been blessed with a balmy, sunny summer. We had basked in the welcoming warmth of scores of strangers—reports of standoffish Mainers notwithstanding. And we had learned a bit about them.

There were places we missed, to be sure, which is what happens when you have the almost-unheard-of luxury of sailing purely where whim, wind, and wanderlust dictate. We had set for ourselves the simple goal—and not an especially onerous one at that—of sailing 236 miles in one summer and completing the course from Quoddy to Kittery. In the end *Consolation*'s log showed that we had sailed 1600 miles, but that was due to the peculiarly spiked nature of Maine's "drowned" coastline and to the 127 stops we'd made.

Dicken, Eliza, Betsy, and I scrubbed our beloved *Consolation* until she gleamed, preparatory to returning her to Fred and Joyce. We were secured on a guest mooring at the Portland Yacht Club, Falmouth Foreside, Maine. Our exploration was at an end, but the subliminal substance of our summer together, I knew, would stay with each of us for some time to come. We'd had an opportunity few families get to enjoy. Amid the hubbub of modern life, we had slowly and happily explored a magnificent stretch of coast, and we were fortunate enough to have done it together as a *family.* The fact that some of that exploration was inward-looking didn't hurt either.

The final disembarkation was, as expected, a melancholy affair. *Hoggie,* little freighter that she is, bore our summer's gear ashore. Betsy, Eliza, and I said our good-byes to Dicken, who sped home to Dalton, and then finished loading our rented car. When nobody was looking, I blew *Consolation* a kiss and silently thanked her for . . . everything.

Some miles down Route 1 we passed a motel with a sign announcing Rooms Available. What the hell, I thought, let's pamper ourselves. I turned in and stopped in front of the office. Thoughts of dry, clean sheets, our own hot shower, a warm swimming pool, and perhaps a movie on television made me ignore the inflated price of the room.

While Betsy and I took turns in the steaming shower, Eliza played with some new-found friends in the pool. Later she came back in and turned on a cartoon show on television. Betsy and I read on the (motionless) bed, but we both found it hard to concentrate on our books. Eliza soon lost interest in the cartoon and turned it off, which surprised me.

"What's wrong, Eliza?" I asked.

"Nothing."

"No, really, do you feel okay?"

"I'm okay."

"What is it then?" Betsy asked.

"I guess I just miss being on *Consolation.*"

BIBLIOGRAPHY

The Audubon Society Field Guide to the Natural Places of the Northeast: Coastal. New York: The Hilltown Press, Inc., 1984.

Block Island to the Canadian Border. Needham, Mass.: Chart Kit/Better Boating Association, Inc., 1991.

Bolton, Charles Knowles. *The Real Founders of New England.* Boston: F.W. Faxon & Company, 1929.

Brace, Gerald Warner. *Between Wind and Water.* New York: W.W. Norton & Company, 1966.

Caldwell, Bill. *Islands of Maine: Where America Really Began.* Portland, Me.: Guy Gannett Publishing Company, 1981.

Carson, Rachel. *The Edge of the Sea.* Boston: Houghton Mifflin Company, 1955.

Clark, Charles E. *Maine: A History.* Hanover, N.H.: University Press of New England, 1990.

Conkling, Philip W. *Islands in Time.* Camden, Me.: Down East Books, 1981.

Dibner, Martin, and George Tice. *Seacoast Maine: People and Places.* Gardiner, Me.: Harpswell Press, 1987.

Doolittle, Duane, ed. *Only in Maine: The Second Down East Reader.* Camden, Me.: Down East Books, 1969.

Duncan, Roger F., and John P. Ware. *A Cruising Guide to the New England Coast.* New York: Dodd, Mead & Company, 1968.

Edey, Maitland A., and the staff of Time-Life Books. *The Northeast Coast.* The American Wilderness Series. New York: Time-Life Books, 1972.

Eliot, Charles W. *John Gilley, One of the Forgotten Millions.* Bar Harbor, Me.: Acadia Press, 1989. [Originally published in 1904 under the title, *John Gilley, Maine Farmer and Fisherman.*]

Ellis, Ray, and Walter Cronkite. *North by Northeast.* Birmingham, Al.: Oxmoor House, 1986.

Fardelmann, Charlotte. *Islands Down East: A Visitor's Guide.* Camden, Me.: Down East Books, 1984.

Gosner, Kenneth L. *A Field Guide to the Atlantic Seashore.* Boston: Houghton Mifflin Company, 1978.

Gould, John. *Maine Lingo: Boiled Owls, Billdads, & Wazzats.* Camden, Me.: Down East Books, 1975.

Graff, Nancy Price, and Richard Howard. *The Call of the Running Tide: A Portrait of an Island Family.* Boston: Little, Brown and Company, 1992.

Griffin, Arthur, and David McCord. *New England Revisited.* Winchester, Mass.: Arthur Griffin, 1966.

Jeffery, David, and Kevin Fleming. "Maine's Working Coast." *National Geographic,* vol. 168 (February 1985): 208–41.

Jewett, Sarah Orne. *The Country of the Pointed Firs and Other Stories.* New York: Doubleday, 1989.

———. *A Country Doctor.* New York: New American Library, 1986.

Ledbetter, Jack. *Maine: The Coast and Islands.* New York: Rizzoli, 1989.

Loomis, Alfred F. *Ranging the Maine Coast.* New York: W.W. Norton & Company, 1939.

McLane, Charles. *Islands of the Mid-Maine Coast.* Vol. 3. Rockland, Me.: Island Institute and Tilbury House Publishers, 1992.

The Maine Atlas and Gazetteer. Freeport, Me.: DeLorme Mapping Company, 1989.

Maloney, Elbert S. *Chapman Piloting Seamanship and Small Boat Handling, 60th ed.* New York: Hearst Marine Books, 1991.

Monegain, Bernie. *A Guide to Exploring Maine's Islands.* Freeport, Me.: DeLorme Mapping Company, 1988.

Ogilvie, Elisabeth. *My World Is an Island.* Camden, Me.: Down East Books, 1990.

Peterson, Roger Tory. *A Field Guide to the Birds.* Boston: Houghton Mifflin Company, 1980.

Porter, Eliot. *Maine.* Boston: Bullfinch Press. Little, Brown & Co., 1986.

Pratt, Charles. *Here on the Island: Being an Account of the Way of Life Several Miles off the Coast of Maine.* New York: Harper & Row, 1974.

Price, Roger W., and the Staff of *Maine Times. Maine Almanac And Book Of Lists.* Topsham, Me.: *Maine Times, Inc.,* 1991.

Rich, Louise Dickinson. *The Coast of Maine, An Informal History and Guide.* New York: Thomas Y. Crowell Company, 1956.

———. *The Peninsula.* New York: J.B. Lippincott, 1958.

———. *State O' Maine.* New York: Harper & Row, 1964.

Richardson, Eleanor Motley. *Hurricane Island: The Town That Disappeared.* Rockland, Me.: Island Institute, 1989.

Roberts, Kenneth, with illus. by N.C. Wyeth. *Trending into Maine.* Boston: Little, Brown & Co., 1938.

Rogers, Donna K. *Tales of Matinicus Island.* Matincus, Me.: Offshore Publishing, 1990.

Simpson, Dorothy. *The Maine Islands in Story and Legend.* New York: J.B. Lippincott, 1960.

Skow, John. *Using the Old L.L. Bean. Sports Illustrated,* vol. 63 (December 2, 1985): 84.

Spectre, Peter H., and Benjamin Mendlowitz. *A Passage in Time.* New York: W.W. Norton & Company, 1991.

Stone, Roger D. *The Voyage of the Sonderling.* New York: Alfred A. Knopf, 1990.

Taft, Hank, and Jan Taft. *A Cruising Guide to the Maine Coast.* Camden, Me.: International Marine Publishing Company, 1988.

Waters, John F. *Exploring New England Shores: A Beachcomer's Handbook.* Lexington, Mass.: Stone Wall Press, 1974.

White, Joel, and Benjamin Mendlowitz. *Wood, Water & Light.* New York: W.W. Norton & Company, 1988.